Pathways to Development

The puzzle of why some countries are more developed than others continues to confound students and practitioners of development alike. Whereas earlier grand explanations focused on issues of 'geography' or 'institutions', the second decade of the twenty-first century finally saw 'politics' arrive centre stage within international development. This catalysed a search to answer the key question: under what conditions do governments become committed to and capable of delivering development? How can these processes be conceptualized and researched? And what (if anything) can be done to 'get the politics right' for development?

Pathways to Development draws on a major comparative research effort to present new answers to the question of how politics shapes development. It develops and applies a 'power domains' framework across multiple countries in the global south to uncover the political drivers of development across a wide range of policy areas, including economic growth, gender equity, health, and education. Hickey and Sen find that a country's pathway to development is shaped less by institutional type than by the nature of the politics and power relations that underpin these institutions and that shape how they actually function in practice within different policy domains.

Comparative analysis reveals two alternative pathways to developmental outcomes, each of which is specific to particular configurations of power. The first involves a dominant ruling coalition with a strong developmental vision that faces an existential threat from social forces; the second involves competitive settlements within which the short-term vision of ruling elites and the politicization of the public bureaucracy are offset by the presence of strong and coherent coalitions within particular policy domains. Hickey and Sen use these insights to generate innovative, practical suggestions for policy actors seeking to promote inclusive development that are aligned to critical differences in political context.

Pathways to Development

From Politics to Power

Sam Hickey
and
Kunal Sen

OXFORD
UNIVERSITY PRESS

OXFORD
UNIVERSITY PRESS

Great Clarendon Street, Oxford, OX2 6DP,
United Kingdom

Oxford University Press is a department of the University of Oxford.
It furthers the University's objective of excellence in research, scholarship,
and education by publishing worldwide. Oxford is a registered trade mark of
Oxford University Press in the UK and in certain other countries

Published in the United States of America by Oxford University Press
198 Madison Avenue, New York, NY 10016, United States of America

British Library Cataloguing in Publication Data

Data available

Library of Congress Control Number: 2023945419

ISBN 9780198872566

DOI: 10.1093/oso/9780198872566.001.0001

Printed and bound by
CPI Group (UK) Ltd, Croydon, CR0 4YY

Acknowledgements

This book brings together nearly a decade of research undertaken by the Effective States and Inclusive Development research centre (ESID), which was based at the Global Development Institute, University of Manchester, from 2011 until 2020. The early twenty-first century saw a growing focus on politics as a key driver of development processes and outcomes, from new theories of why some nations are wealthier than others through to how development agencies and other actors might work as well as think politically. ESID's aim was to build on this momentum, reframing one of these new theories—political settlements analysis—to help identify the specific political conditions under which political elites became committed and states became capable of delivering development and how this might inform development policy and practice. We took a broad view of inclusive development and investigated a range of different 'policy domains': economic (growth, structural transformation, natural resource governance), social (education, health, women's rights, and social protection) and governance related (public-sector reform and state capacity). Our combined 'power domains' framework was used to undertake in-depth and comparative analysis in sixteen countries across Africa, South America, and South and Southeast Asia by research teams that each combined researchers drawn from these regions as well as from Europe and North America.

This book reports on the work undertaken within the first phase of ESID's work, plus a related project on 'pockets of effectiveness' funded largely by the Economic and Social Research Council (Hickey 2023a). Most of this work has been made available in much longer form in distinct publications, the majority of which were published by Oxford University Press. These publications are fully referenced throughout this book, and we would encourage readers to engage with the extended treatments that they offer of each policy domain. Here we summarize the highlights to offer a platform for making a broader statement about our programme of research can tell us about the politics of inclusive development when taken as a whole. Later work, enabled by a three-year funding extension from the then British government's Department for International Development, developed some of this work further, including on the local politics of social protection (Lavers 2022), urban governance (Goodfellow and Jackman 2023), and a retheorization of political settlements theory (Kelsall et al. 2022). These works are not included here for reasons of timing but also coherence, in that they adopted somewhat different frameworks to ask somewhat different questions.

Our first round of thanks goes to those ESID colleagues who helped us to lead and undertake the research projects reported here and their respective research teams, starting with David Hulme, who as ESID's Chief Executive Officer offered important guidance and inspiration throughout. Next, to our excellent research teams. On *economic growth and development*: Lant Pritchett, Erik Werker, Jonathan Said, Khwima Singini, Mirza Hassan, Selim Raihan, Tim Kelsall, Heng Seiha, Robert Darko Osei, Charles Ackah, George Domfe, Michael Danquah, Badru Bukenya, Pritish Behuria, Tom Goodfellow, Sabyasachi Kar, Jagadish Prasad Sahu, and Matt Tyce; on *natural resource governance*: Tony Bebbington, Abdul-Gafaru Abdulai, Marja Hinfelaar, Denise Humphreys-Bebbington, Cynthia Caborn, Giles Mohan, Abdul-Gafaru Abdulai, Kojo Asante, Badru Bukenya, Angelo Izama, and Haggai Matsiko; on *health*: Tim Kelsall, Simeen Mahmud, Moogdho Mahzab, Nuzhat Sharmeen, Abdul-Gafaru Abdulai, Badru Bukenya, Fred Golooba-Mutebi, Yvonne Habiyonezeye; on *education*: Naomi Hossain, Mirza Hasan, Tim Williams, Brian Levy, Edward Ampratwum, Mohammed Awal, Franklin Oduro, Md Ashikur Rahman, Khondoker Shakhawat Ali, M. Sajidul Islam, Robert Cameron, Ursula Hoadley, Vinothan Naidoo, Tim Kelsall, Sothy Khieng, Chuong Chantha, Tieng Tek Muy, Anne Mette Kjær, Nansozi K. Muwanga, and David Jackman; on *women's rights*: Sohela Nazneen, Amon Mwiine, Josephien Aikhire, Jennie E. Burnet, Lillian Artz, Valérie Grand'Maison, Beatrix Allah-Mensah, Rhoda Osei-Afful, Asmita Basu, and Eleni Sifaki; on *social protection*: Tom Lavers, Abdul-Gafaru Abdulai, Fred Wanyama, Anna McCord, Badru Bukenya, and Benjamin Chemouni; and, on *public-sector governance* and *pockets of effectiveness*: Abdul-Gafaru Abdulai, Badru Bukenya, William Muhumuza, Pablo Yanguas Gil, Caesar Cheelo, Benjamin Chemouni, Marja Hinfelaar, Pritish Behuria, Haggai Matsiko, Giles Mohan, and Matt Tyce. Clearly, special mention is required for Abdul-Gafaru Abdulai and Badru Bukenya, who delivered on numerous fronts for ESID regarding their respective countries of Ghana and Uganda, and who continue to be valued friends and colleagues. In addition, a succession of excellent research associates cycled through ESID over its near decade of existence, adding great value to our work in general as well to as the specific projects listed above. Many thanks to Badru Bukenya, Pablo Yanguas Gil, Phillip Green, David Jackman, Sophie King, Chris Lyon, Kate Pruce, Farwa Sial, and Cathy Wilcox. Special thanks to Chris Lyon for his work in helping to collate and deliver this manuscript and to Clare Cummings for supporting the final and much-belated push to get it over the line.

We were privileged to be joined on this journey by some outstanding scholars who have been critical friends throughout, acting as advisors, attending ESID workshops, conferences, and conference presentations, hosting us at seminars, reviewing and challenging our work, and generally making things even more interesting and convivial than they might otherwise have been. Special thanks to David Booth, Melanie Cammett, Pilar Domingo, Peter Evans, Anne Marie Goetz, Duncan Green, Merilee Grindle, Emmanuel Gyimah-Boadi, Barbara Harriss-White, Daniel Honig, Martha Johnson, Emily Jones, Ha Choon Chang, Karuti Kanyinga, Peter Lewis, Heather Marquette, Celestin Monga, Erin McDonnell, Helena Perez Nino, Jon Phillips, James Robinson, Michael Roll, Ben Ross Schneider, Nicolai Schulz, Prerna Singh, Julia Strauss, Nic van de Walle, Georgina Waylen, and Jennifer Widner. Scores of hard-working academics conducted anonymous peer reviews of our working papers, greatly enhancing the quality of our analysis and finished products—many thanks indeed.

We also benefited from the feedback we received at the many conferences and workshops where we presented our work over the years and we would like to thank all those scholars generous enough to attend and organize the numerous sessions workshops through which our work got discussed and improved. This includes successive annual conferences of the African Studies Association (UK and USA), UK Development Studies Association, and the American and UK Political Science Associations respectively, and colleagues at the School of Advanced International Studies (Johns Hopkins University), the Centre of African Studies (Edinburgh University), the Centre for Development Studies (University of Cambridge), the Department of International Development (London School of Economics), the Watson School (Brown University), the department of political science at the Massachusetts Institute for Technology, and numerous presentations to advisors at development agencies, most notably the UK Department for International Development and the World Bank.

Our final academic debts are to the hundreds of anonymous experts who responded to our survey questions and agreed to be interviewed for the many research projects that ESID undertook. Your insights provide the core of our work, and both these and the time you were prepared to offer to us are deeply appreciated.

Many colleagues at Manchester have assisted with the management of this project, organizing workshops, handling budgets, copy-editing papers, and doing all the other administrative work required to make collaborative research happen. We are very grateful to Kat Bethell, Julia Brunt, Clare Degenhardt, Julie Rafferty, and Anna Webster. ESID was funded by the then Department for International Development and we benefited from the thoughtful and hands-off support of successive 'handlers': our thanks to Max Everest Phillips, Helen Richards, Zaza Curran, Peter Evans, and David Pedley. Many thanks also to Adam Swallow at Oxford University Press for supporting this project from the outset and to his colleagues for guiding it through contracting and production.

Finally, we dedicate this book to the memory of Adrian Leftwich, an inspirational and much-missed colleague.

Sam Hickey
Manchester, October 2022
Kunal Sen
Helsinki and Manchester, October 2022

Contents

List of Figures

List of Tables

1
Pathways to Development
Introduction

Puzzles and an Argument

Under what conditions do governments become committed to and capable of delivering development? The dominant answer to this question within international development since the late twentieth century has focused primarily on the role of institutions. The underlying assumption has been that the further that countries travel towards developing liberal economic and political institutions—involving free-market economies, rules-based governance, and democratic competition for power—the greater their chances of achieving economic growth and human development. But is this broad proposition a useful one and does it hold in the face of the available evidence? Many observers have now concluded that it is politics, rather than institutions, that constitutes the key driver of different development trajectories in the global south. Leading development scholars and the main international development agencies alike emphasize that 'it's the politics stupid' and have devised new theoretical and strategic approaches through which to identify and address the multiple ways in which politics shapes progress (North, Wallis, and Weingast (NWW) 2009; 2013; Acemoglu and Robinson 2012, 2019; World Bank 2017). However, it remains largely unclear as to what forms of politics really matter, how these can be conceptualized, and what (if anything) can be done to 'get the politics right' for development.

Moreover, the puzzle is not simply one of trying to explain why some countries perform better than others in terms of aggregate levels of development; to this must be added the question of why some countries perform so unevenly across the different development challenges they face. Why do some countries excel at generating rapid economic growth whilst struggling to deliver services? Why are some countries committed and able to govern their natural resources effectively while failing to protect the rights of their most vulnerable citizens? The question of why some countries have much greater capacity and commitment to deliver on domestic development challenges

Pathways to Development. Sam Hickey and Kunal Sen, Oxford University Press.
 DOI: 10.1093/oso/9780198872566.003.0001

is arguably of greater importance to citizens of those countries than how they are faring compared to other countries, but it is one that development scholars are only now starting to grapple with (Centeno et al. 2017).

In this book we explore these questions by examining a number of puzzles that continue to vex both students and practitioners of development. Why, for example, do some countries avoid the so-called natural resource 'curse' while others do not? The dominant answer to this puzzle has generally been that countries with the stronger and more democratic institutions in place at the time that natural resources are discovered will be better placed to govern these resources in the national interest (Rosser 2006; Ross 2012). However, when we compare two developing countries that discovered similar quantities of oil at a similar point in time—namely, Ghana and Uganda in the mid-2000s—this proposition does not seem to hold. On paper, Ghana is ahead of Uganda on virtually every indicator of economic and political development, including all standard measures of good governance and democracy. However, when we investigated how each country was governing its new-found oil wealth, we found that Uganda seemed to be doing a better job than Ghana in important respects, including securing higher returns from international oil companies, strengthening the regulatory environment, and taking steps to avoid the resource curse. The highly competitive political environment within which Ghana's governing elites operate seemed to be reducing their commitment to putting in place rules to govern oil and to protecting the capacity of bureaucrats to perform their role. The opposite seemed to be occurring in Uganda, where a more 'dominant' leader with longer-term horizons invested in building and protecting a bureaucratic 'pocket of effectiveness' capable of governing the oil sector in the national interest.

A different puzzle of contemporary development in the global south—the rapid rise of cash transfers as a solution to problems of poverty and vulnerability—led us to explore the conditions under which governments become committed to protecting their poorest citizens through offering them social assistance. Again, our investigations yielded some surprising results that challenged mainstream interpretations of how social welfare policies become embedded. First, we found that the rise of cash transfers could not be explained simply as a donor-driven development: domestic political dynamics emerged as having the definitive influence over the level and type of elite commitment to social assistance that we observed. It was only when the policy ideas being promoted by external actors became aligned with the ideas and incentives of ruling elites that cash transfers took hold. Second, neither the level of economic growth nor the level of democracy offered a useful predictor of how swiftly and extensively governments in Africa would come to distribute cash transfers from the mid-2000s onwards. Specific elections did play a positive role in driving political support for cash transfers in Kenya and to some extent in Zambia, but we also found that less democratic countries, such as Ethiopia and Rwanda, were amongst the best performers. What seemed to matter here was not so much the level of economic growth or level of democracy—or the extent of pressure from donor agencies—but rather the extent to which those in power perceived themselves to be vulnerable to threats from either ordinary citizens and/or their elite rivals for power, and whether they saw cash transfers as helping to deal with that threat. This cut across the more or less democratic countries we looked at, whereby the greater the extent of the perceived threat within the ruling coalition, and the stronger the fit with an ideological project, the swifter and more extensive the policy response.

The picture became more nuanced still when we tried to assess a third challenge, namely how governments that have successfully improved access to services for a significant proportion of their population could go on to improve the *quality* of such services. In the context of education, making the shift from 'schooling to learning' has proved particularly difficult for developing countries (Pritchett 2013), despite earlier successes in ensuring that the majority of their school-age populations, including girls, attend primary school. Our research in six cases revealed two political economy explanations for the learning crisis. First, the coalitions that support the expansion of school provision (including populist leaders, their rural constituencies, teachers' unions, and aid agencies) are more powerful than those supporting learning outcomes (which are largely confined to business groups and middle-class parents). The imbalance of power between these coalitions in most developing countries generates clear incentives for governing elites to improve access to education rather than undertake the difficult work of improving the quality of provision. Second, we found that neither the competitive politics of a country like Ghana nor the developmental dominance apparent in Rwanda had led to any serious effort to improve the quality of education, with both types of government continuing to undermine this prospect through populist policy measures. However, whereas some less democratic governments seemed to be doing a better job at managing natural resources and delivering social assistance than more democratic ones, we found the opposite. When it comes to delivering higher quality education, the greater the concentration of power in the executive, and the more hierarchical the governance arrangements, the weaker the policy response. Our research suggested that the answer to this puzzle might lie in how well different political contexts are capable of dealing with specific policy challenges. Ensuring that children learn in schools involves a complex and transactional system of governance that cannot be delivered by executive fiat and top-down pressures alone. Where we did find rising levels of commitment and capacity to improve learning, this was usually at the local level, and often seemed to have little to do with regime type per se. Rather, it was the work of local coalitions committed to devise 'institutional fixes' that could work around dominant incentives and ideas that generated successful educational outcomes.

The final puzzle we consider at this point of the volume revolves around the question of why some parts of the state seem to function very effectively in developing countries whilst others generally fail to deliver on their mandate. So called 'pockets of effectiveness' or PoEs are often cast as harbingers of how rules-based forms of governance may emerge in developing countries otherwise mired in the politics of patronage. However, in the eighteen PoEs that we examined across five different countries, we found that organizational effectiveness required a mixture of political loyalty and bureaucratic competence rather than the displacement of patronage by pure forms of meritocracy. All our public sector organizations struggled in the face of competitive pressures and the incentives that this created to misuse them for political gain; they were only able to offset these pressures when certain conditions enabled political rulers with a defined ideological project to forge coalitions with like-minded and loyal bureaucrats, usually with external support. However, more dominant political rulers will tend not to protect public sector organizations as part of a wider process of state-building unless they perceive themselves to be facing a threat to which building durable and impartial bureaucratic institutions constitutes a rational response.

In these four policy domains—and the others that we researched and report on here, including economic growth, women's empowerment and health—we found little evidence to support an institutionalist reading of how different countries approached different development challenges. Instead, we found that a country's pathway to development was shaped less by institutional type than by the nature of the politics and power relations that underpinned these institutions and which shape how they actually function in practice. The power relations between different elite groups and coalitions competing for power, and the different ideas that bind them together, are particularly important here, as are the relationships between governing coalitions and their support base in society. True, these relationships are often mediated through institutions. But it is the balance and nature of the power relations themselves that matters most, and which until recently have been largely overlooked within development theory. In this volume we draw on recent theoretical advances within the broader turn to taking politics seriously to argue that development trajectories in the global south must be understood with reference to the 'political settlement' that prevails in specific contexts, whereby a political settlement refers to the balance of power between contending social groups (Khan 2017; Kelsall 2018). Here our work is in line with recent and compelling efforts to reframe the politics of development in terms of contemporary political and social forces (e.g. Centeno et al. 2017), particularly in the form of coalitions (Teichman 2015).

Going further, we suggest that it is possible to identify different *types* of political settlement, and that these different types of settlement offer different prospects and pathways to development depending on the policy challenge at hand. The key distinctions here relate to the configuration of both *social* and *political* power within a settlement (Kelsall et al. 2022), and the ideas that bind elites together within it. In terms of the social configuration of power, which social groups do elites need to worry about in terms of their capacity to disrupt political order and regime continuity (Doner et al. 2005; Slater 2010)? The perception among elites that they needed to respond to certain perceived threats and demands from particular social constituencies is critical to understanding not only how much governments will invest in providing both public and private goods—as with education and cash transfers—but also who gets these goods and the effort placed on ensuring the quality of these goods. However, the capacity of coalitions to deliver on their commitments is strongly mediated by the configuration of political power, which refers to how elites compete for power and the coherence of coalitions in power. Here we can distinguish between political settlements in developing countries where ruling coalitions are coherent and dominant in their hold on power and those that face credible competition from rival elite factions (Khan 2010; Whitfield et al. 2015). Where competition for political power among elites is high, but the institutions established to mediate this conflict and govern resources remain weak, this will tend to increase the incentives of those in power to use public office primarily as a means of maintain themselves in power, and to distribute resources and opportunities in return for political loyalty. In contrast, rulers in more dominant settlements, particularly where the social configuration of power incentivizes a redistributive and protective approach, may be more inclined to adopt a longer-term perspective and to invest in building institutions and development for the long run.

Finally, our research also suggests that elite commitment to development and state building is driven by ideas as well as incentives and self-interest. Indeed, elite perceptions of self-interest such as their sense of systemic threats to their political survival are, of course, ideational in nature rather than constituting interests that are in any sense 'objective'. Other paradigmatic ideas that we identify as powerful in holding political settlements and developmental coalitions together include ideologies of nationalism, self-reliance, and various versions of developmentalism, suggesting the need to go beyond rational actor versions of political behaviour.

The recognition that democratic processes are not necessarily conducive to development is well supported in a wide range of literature, including on developmental states (e.g. Leftwich 1994; Haggard 2018), women's rights (Waylen 2014), and educational progress (Pritchett 2019), and our acknowledgement of this here is not intended to undermine the broader case for democracy. The specific problem that we identify here is with what have become termed 'competitive clientelist' political settlements (Khan 2010; Levy 2014), with reference to contexts within which formal institutions for political competition become integrated with informal institutions characterized by patron–client politics. The problem is not one with democracy per se but rather with the ways in which the competition for political power interacts with institutions and the unintended consequences this often produces. More specifically, in conditions where historical processes of state formation and structural transformation remain nascent, intense processes of competition can undermine rather than reinforce moves towards more rules-based forms of governance, in the short run at least (Grindle 2012). Our key point here is not to reignite the long-standing debate over whether democratic or authoritarian forms of governance are the most developmental, but rather to join others in suggesting that this debate has been hinged in the wrong place (Kelsall 2014). The focus on the form that institutions take, rather than on how underlying forms of politics and power shape how they actually function, has diverted our attention from the more important drivers of development.

Our finding that dominant political settlements perform poorly in terms of improving the quality of social provisioning and that competitive political settlements also generate incentives to provide some public goods to citizens (see Chapter Five) reinforces these points. This in turn emphasizes the need for more nuanced understanding of how politics, power, and institutions interact to produce different levels of capacity and commitment to delivering different forms of development. Different kinds of political settlement offer different pathways to development: this is an important finding and supports calls for external interventions to be more closely aligned to the incentives and opportunities generated by these different types of political settlement (Levy 2014; Kelsall et al. 2022).

Going further, we argue that governing elites operating within different types of political settlement also seem to deal with different kinds of policy challenge in different ways. In particular, dominant political settlements seem to struggle with policy challenges that are 'transactional' rather than 'logistical' in nature (Andrews et al. 2012). Transactional policy challenges—such as ensuring that children are actually learning while they are in school—involve multiple interactions between politicians, service providers, and citizens at many levels. This in turn requires that multiple flows of information are in operation and that space exists for problem-solving alliances and coalitions to be built. Such conditions are more difficult to achieve in dominant political settlements, which face the additional constraint of policy failures caused by inadequate oversight mechanisms and the political difficulties of reversing earlier policy commitments.

Political settlements, then, strongly shape the development trajectories that countries take by shaping capacity and commitment across a range of policy areas. Dominant and competitive types of political settlement tend to achieve different rates of progress and to deliver development in different ways, depending in part on the nature of the policy challenge to hand. Dominant settlements may offer better prospects for rapid progress, particularly with regards to logistical policy challenges (such as delivering access to education), but they can also be subject to the whims of capricious leaders, struggle with transactional policy challenges (such as improving the quality of education), and find it difficult to deal with policy failures and reversals. In contrast, competitive settlements may deliver steadier progress and space for innovation, particularly with more transactional policy challenges, while lacking the enforcement capacities required for rapid progress. What is important, then, is to gain deeper understandings not only of how different types of political settlement shape the levels of development that countries achieve but of how each offers different pathways to achieving development within different policy domains. This matters for development strategy as well as for development theory. Neither the broad policy prescriptions of the good-governance agenda, derived from cross-sectional data analysis on which types of institutions are broadly correlated with development (Khan 2005), nor the resort to 'context matters' and 'everywhere is different', provide useful guides to action. Our use of comparative case-study analysis to identify the different pathways to development that are characteristic of different types of political settlement helps to ensure that policy responses can be more closely attuned to the specific drivers of development in particular types of context. For example, we find that, whereas it may be possible to undertake system-wide processes of reform in dominant settlements where elite commitment to reform exists, the best first step within the often 'noisier' world of competitive clientelism might be to start building coalitions for change that can devise the kinds of solutions required to work around the constraints that elite-level power struggles can place on institutions. We also find that the strong emphasis on accountability in international development since the late twentieth century needs to be joined by an equally strong focus on state capacity, as suggested in Sustainable Development Goal 16 on governance, which focuses on building institutions that are 'effective' as well as 'inclusive'. Whether states can perform is determined not only by long-run processes of institutional development, as often shaped by colonial legacies, but also by the configurations of power that prevail in contemporary settings (Centeno et al. 2017). This suggests possibilities for building innovative forms of state capacity, and for delivering on particular development challenges, including in the form of 'bureaucratic pockets of effectiveness' (Roll 2014; and see Chapter 6). Taking these lessons seriously would mean international development agencies moving beyond their current lip service to the 'politics-matters' discourse, undertaking steps to embed political analysis within their institutional practices and ensuring that their interventions are closely attuned to the political dynamics at work within particular types of context. Our finding that ideas matter opens further points of intervention for development agencies that are today as important for their role as knowledge brokers as development financiers.

This volume makes the case for both thinking and working differently with regards the politics of development through the following steps. Chapter 2 sets our contribution in theoretical context and introduces the 'power domains' approach as a new way to conceptualize the politics of development. The focus here is on how political settlements as a domain of power shape the capacity and commitment to deliver development in specific domains of development policy. In the subsequent four chapters we apply this framework to the types of development puzzles introduced above—namely, those involving economic growth and the natural resource curse (Chapter 3); efforts to protect vulnerable groups through cash transfers and to protect the rights of women through passing anti-domestic violence legislation (Chapter 4); the challenges of reducing maternal mortality and providing higher-quality education through social-service provision (Chapter 5), and, finally, the puzzle of achieving more effective and accountable forms of governance, including through pockets of bureaucratic effectiveness (Chapter 6). Chapter 7 summarizes the overall argument and points towards the implications for further research and development strategy. The Appendices include details of the comparative research projects that lie behind the abbreviated summaries presented here and brief sketches of the political settlement dynamics within the key countries where the research was undertaken. First, the next section briefly charts the rise of the turn to politics within international development theory and practice to help place this book within its intellectual and strategic context.

The Rise of Politics in International Development

The puzzle of why some countries are wealthier and more developed than others continues to confound students and practitioners of development alike. Whereas earlier grand explanations focused on issues of 'geography' or 'institutions', the second decade of the twenty-first century finally saw politics arrive centre stage within international development. Influential scholars who had previously identified 'institutions' as determining why some countries are wealthier than others now placed politics at the centre of their theories (NWW 2009; Acemoglu and Robinson 2012, 2019). The world of development policy has also made significant, if incomplete, steps towards 'thinking and working politically' (Carothers and de Gramont 2013), with a growing number of agencies undertaking political economy analyses to inform their engagements and recent development reports drawing heavily on the language and sensibilities of the new turn to taking politics seriously (World Bank 2017).[1]

This should not be surprising; politics is fundamentally about contestation over resources and ideas: about who gets what, how, and why (Leftwich 1994). However, politics has rarely been central to mainstream development theory and practice in the post-war era, for a series of reasons that include ideological and institutional constraints (Leftwich 2005; Hickey 2008). For example, calls to 'bring politics back into development' were made frequently during the 1980s and 1990s (Goldsworthy 1988; Leftwich 1994), often in relation to the rapid progress being made by developmental states in East Asia (Johnson 1982; Evans 1995; Leftwich 1995). However, such calls arrived while neoliberal sensibilities were taking hold, and accounts that put politics and the state at the centre of development theory and practice, as opposed to the role of markets, were actively downplayed by powerful development agencies in favour of protecting the new hegemony (Wade 1996). Although this move reduced the influence of the developmental states literature, and of other work on the political origins of (under)development being undertaken at the time (e.g. Bates 1981), the developmental state literature helped inspire

[1] See http://doingdevelopmentdifferently.com/ and https://twpcommunity.org/.

a wider range of scholarship on the politics of development, including comparative historical work that focused on how elite perceptions of 'systemic vulnerability' and underlying state–society alignments shaped whether institutions would be developmental or not (e.g. Doner et al. 2005; Slater 2010; see Haggard 2018 for a summary).

When a stronger sense of politics was incorporated into international development during the 1990s and early 2000s, however, the inspiration was not from these strands of political analysis but rather from new institutional economics. Moving on from the idea that development primarily involved processes of capital accumulation, new institutionalism directed attention to the long-term evolution of the 'rules of the game' within which actors operate, how they shape development trajectories, and particularly the behavioural incentives for elite groups that are embedded in different kinds of rules (North 1990). Rodrik (2004) shows how neo-institutionalist economics influenced mainstream thinking on 'good governance' during the 1990s, as with the marked convergence around the assumption that certain institutions (e.g. secure property rights) are central to achieving economic development. The good-governance agenda that emerged during this period emphasized not only the streamlining of the central state (e.g. decentralization, public-sector reform) and the promotion of inclusive and accountable liberal institutions (including elections, anti-corruption commissions, and so on), but also placed a major emphasis on the role of civil society, social capital, and citizens to promote such institutions.

By the mid-2000s, the tide had shifted towards politics playing a more central role in the theory and practice of international development (Leftwich 2005), driven in part by the growing level of problems facing the good-governance agenda. Long opposed from different perspectives (Khan 1995; Potter 2000; Grindle 2004), even development agencies were now aware that promoting certain types of institutions in developing-country contexts was a highly problematic venture. Successive internal evaluations revealed how large scale and widespread the failures with this agenda had been, particularly in terms of public-sector reforms. One World Bank report found that half of 145 countries with donor-sponsored reforms saw declines in government effectiveness between 1998 and 2008, a finding soon reinforced with similar portfolio reviews of governance work undertaken by other development agencies (Andrews 2013). A central problem was the clash between good-governance ideals and the pressing incentives facing governing elites in developing countries, many of whom spent more time worrying about how to maintain order and keep themselves in power than longer-term goals of state-building and democratization. This realization that elite-level politics is central to how institutions actually function in practice would be the critical insight of the new turn to politics by prominent development scholars, from both long-term critics of new institutionalism (e.g. Khan 2005, 2017) and some of its strongest proponents (NWW 2009; Acemoglu and Robinson 2012).

The political turn in development policy and practice was also informed by the increasing use of experimental methods in political science and in social sciences more broadly (McDermott 2002; Druckman et al. 2011). Experimental methods were increasingly used during the 2000s in evaluations of interventions designed to improve participation in the political and policy process, reduce corruption and leakages, and improve state capacity, and figured prominently in governance research undertaken by major development agencies such as the World Bank (see Khemani et al. 2016).[2] However, experimental methods have been increasingly criticized for their lack of external validity—that is, whether the findings of a particular study could be generalized to other contexts—as well as focusing only on micro-interventions that could be observed only in the short term. Thus, experimental methods are not particularly suitable for addressing broader questions around the deeper structural factors that underlie economic and political underdevelopment. As Deaton and Cartwright (2018: 1) convincingly argue: 'RCTs can play a role in scientific knowledge and useful predictions but they can only do so as part of cumulative program, combining with other methods, including conceptual and theoretical development, to discover not "what works" but "why things work"'.

The political turn has directly informed some important but still incipient shifts within development policy and practice, in what has been appropriately referred to as an 'almost revolution' (Carothers and de Gramont 2013). An emblematic feature of this almost revolution is reflected in the sense that, during the early to mid-2000s, the use of political economy analysis became almost routine in some development agencies, even if more progress is required before it can be said to have become institutionalized (Fritz et al. 2014; Yanguas and Hulme 2015). Development agencies have also moved away from the certainties of the good-governance agenda, and have started to embrace, somewhat tentatively, the principles of an emerging new governance agenda that is based less on grand reforms than on working with locally based teams of reformers to identify solutions to specific problems in a more adaptive and contextually specific way (Andrews et al. 2012). The 2018

[2] A key player in this drive towards the use of experimental methods in governance research was the Poverty Action Lab through its Governance Initiative; see https://www.povertyactionlab.org/GI.

World Development Report on *Governance and the Law* catches some of these shifts, employing the language of the new theoretical turn to politics, with its emphasis on 'elite bargaining' and 'political settlements', and the new sense in which the normative project of promoting certain forms of 'best-practice' institutions has now been shelved in favour of a more realist, 'best-fit' approach (Andrews 2013). This has apparently pushed the mainstream further away from the certainties of the 'good-governance' agenda, displaced by a somewhat sombre account of the prospects for institutional reform in contexts where elite political behaviour is depicted in more realist terms than was apparent in the earlier emphasis on national 'ownership' (Booth 2011).

The (overdue) rise of politics within international development, then, has made impressive progress during the first two decades of the twenty first century. However, this 'almost revolution' has left several important questions unanswered:

- Which forms of politics matter most in shaping development progress, both between and within countries? Evidence gaps and a lack of theory-testing mean that we do not have clear answers to this question, in part because the new theories of how politics shapes development have not been trialled and tested in developing-country contexts in a systematic way.
- Missing middle: as Grindle (2017) notes, there is large gap between the macro and micro advances that have been made around the new politics and governance agenda since the 2010s, with little sense of what relationship there might be between the forms of politics identified in new theories of long-run development and either new experimental data or the techniques and ambitions of the new 'doing development differently' agenda. For example:
    - How do deep-run processes of politics and institutional development play out within the shorter-time periods within which decision-makers operate?
    - Do underlying forms of politics and power relations play out in the same way across different sectors or domains of policy (e.g. economic growth or social provisioning), or is there a specific politics to these domains that also needs to be accounted for?

Seeking answers to these questions, through a theoretical and methodological approach that can hopefully be used more broadly, is the core objective of this book.

2

Reconceptualizing the Politics of Development

The Power Domains Approach

The first decade of the twenty-first century, then, saw the emergence of a shift from 'institutions matter' to 'politics matters' within discussions of why some countries have managed to achieve higher levels of economic and political progress than others. A key focus within this newly politicized body of development theory has been on the role of elites and inter-elite bargaining in shaping how institutions actually function in terms of the distribution of resources and status within society. This chapter critically discusses some of the main propositions emerging from this literature before setting out a conceptual approach—namely, a 'power domains' perspective, which seeks to build on the strengths of the new theoretical turn to politics. Our specific aim is to develop political settlements analysis in ways that move it beyond a narrow focus on elite incentives to incorporate a stronger appreciation of the role played by both ideas and broader social groupings in shaping the configuration of power within which elites operate. By linking this form of political settlements analysis to specific policy domains via our 'power domains' perspective, we can investigate contemporary development puzzles that have to date been overlooked within the *longue durée* remit of much institutionalist analysis. The final job of this chapter is to set out the methodological approach that we used to explore how power domains shape the capacity and commitment to deliver development in a range of different policy areas.

From New Institutional Economics to the Politics of Elite Bargaining and State–Society Relations

In the 1980s and 1990s, disenchantment with the limitations of neoclassical economics in understanding how real-world markets function, especially in the developing world, catalysed the emergence of New Institutional Economics (NIE). A growing body of empirical research showed that

Pathways to Development. Sam Hickey and Kunal Sen, Oxford University Press.
 DOI: 10.1093/oso/9780198872566.003.0002

institutions, understood as 'the rules of the game' in a society, are central to the understanding of why some economies have performed better than others (Hall and Jones 1999; Acemoglu et al. 2001; Rodrik et al. 2004). While NIE had several strands, the common tenet in this body of work was the emphasis placed on transactions costs and imperfect information in understanding market failures in developing countries—according to NIE, institutions that evolve to lower transactions costs are key to the performance of economies (North 1990, 1998). NIE was highly influential among policy actors working on transitional and developing economies at the time, in recognition that market reforms were unlikely to be successful if the appropriate institutions that support economic activity and distribute its benefits (Rodrik 2004) were not in place. A slew of agency publications focused on the significance of institutions for economic growth and development progress more broadly (World Bank 2002; DFID 2003; IMF 2005). However, NIE soon became subject to growing criticism from a range of quarters. Particular problems were raised with the apparent difficulty that the approach had in dealing with issues of redistributive institutional change, particularly involving issues of collective action and class conflict (Bardhan 1989; Khan 1995), the role of elites in maintaining dysfunctional institutions over time (Leftwich 2007), and the lack of sociological depth in explanations of how institutions emerged and changed over time (Portes 2006). By the mid-2000s, erstwhile proponents of new institutionalism had moved towards a more consciously politicized reading of development. Importantly, this focused less on institutional legacies per se than on their interaction with elite-level relations of power. For North, Wallis, and Weingast, 'political and economic development result from creating more sophisticated and durable institutions to structure elite relations within the dominant coalition' (NWW 2009: 159); as such, the differences between developed and developing countries is attributable to 'the pattern of social relationships' in each, but particularly within 'the elite'. Mushtaq Khan's work (2000, 2010, 2017) on political settlements adopts a similar perspective, whereby the 'political settlement' refers to 'the balance or distribution of power between contending social groups and social classes, on which any state is based' (di John and Putzel 2009: 4), and is arrived at through a process of struggle and bargaining between elite groups. This settlement establishes the basis for institutional arrangements to take shape; critically, institutions must be arranged to distribute enough resources to powerful organized groups in society, to ensure their acquiescence in maintaining order (Khan 2010: 4). Taken together, these approaches suggest two main and interrelated transmission mechanisms through which limited-access orders and political settlements shape developmental forms of state capacity and elite commitment. The first flows from the stability of institutional arrangements, the second from the nature of ruling coalitions. Political stability and order are critical, not only in allowing institutions to function, but by enabling ruling elites to engage in the longer-term thinking and planning required for investments in building growth-enhancing institutions. Where elites are constantly struggling to assert their legitimacy and that of a prevailing order, the incentives are to undertake short-term measures designed to maintain order and keep the regime in power. In a context of personalized deals between elites, this involves both creating rent-seeking possibilities for potentially troublesome elites and securing their support for 'limited-access' (and usually clientelist) institutional arrangements that can help offer greater returns than they could attain through violent means (NWW 2009).[1]

The more distinctive contribution of this new wave of thinking concerns the role played by *coalitions* in shaping state capacity and elite commitment. From a political settlements perspective, the 'ruling coalition' is the pre-eminent form of political organization in a given context, and the nature of this coalition is critical to developmental orientation and outcomes. The proposed causality here runs from the configuration of power through institutions to development, with political coalitions acting as the mechanism through which these relationships are mediated (e.g. Portes 2006; Poteete 2009). The specific ways in which this happens depends on the wider field of power relations within which ruling coalitions are located and how they navigate this. There are also clear echoes here of Mancur Olson's discussion (1993) of elites as 'bandits', and Robert Bates's proposition (1981) that the challenge of making developmentally effective policies in Africa lay in the capture of the state apparatus by a narrow social group, whose interests were at odds with those of the primary producers on which African economies largely rely. Perhaps the clearest precursor of political settlements theory is Margaret Levi's seminal work (1988) on the politics of why there are systematic differences in revenue production policies across states. Levi takes the institutional configuration of a society as a function of the relative bargaining power of ruling elites, where relative bargaining power is a function of coercive, economic, and political resources.

Reflecting earlier work on developmental states (e.g. Evans 1995; Khan 2010) argues that the productive capacities of capitalists and the types of relationships that they have with the political elite will strongly shape the ways and extent to which ruling coalitions invest in economic growth-enhancing institutions. This focus on the interactions between politics, institutions,

[1] This paragraph is borrowed from Hickey et al. (2015).

and the political economy constitutes one of the more distinctive contributions of political settlements analysis. In particular, Khan notes that, in economies where structural transformation has barely occurred and the economy remains largely informalized, political relationships will inevitably be similarly informal in what he terms 'clientelist' political settlements. If ruling elites are unable to extract sufficient revenue from the formal economy to keep powerful groups content, then the predominant means of maintaining order will be through clientelist means. This marks a critical point of difference between Khan's work and that of both NWW (2009) and Acemoglu and Robinson (2012), who lack the sense of historical political economy that informs political settlements theory (Gray 2016), and who, in their unwillingness to problematize the nature of capitalism and the effects it has on the nature of political order, offer correspondingly weaker insights into the interplay of political economy and politics.[2]

This ontological shift to centre the configuration of power constitutes a significant advance for efforts to theorize the politics of development. Whereas previous accounts of institutional change were limited to long-run accounts of either 'path dependence' or 'diffusion' (Campbell 2004, as cited in Portes 2006), the focus on how inter-elite struggles shape institutional emergence and functioning opens up a further route to understanding how institutions change. In seeking to identify when and how states actually *perform* when it comes to delivering development, Centeno et al. (2017) similarly place a greater emphasis on contemporaneous social and political forces rather than purely historical factors. Importantly, understanding the configuration of elite power may offer more direct insights into how capable and committed ruling elites are to promoting development within short and medium-term timeframes, including the conditions under which they mobilize long-run institutional endowments such as state capacity.

Rethinking Political Settlements Analysis: Incorporating a Sense of the Social and the Ideational

However, problems remain in terms of the reach of this newly politicized body of development theory, in at least three respects (Hickey et al. 2015). The first two involve ontological blind spots, whereby political settlements

[2] We take some of this thinking further in our development of theorizing at the level of the 'policy domain', whereby we conceptualize the domain of accumulation in terms of the 'rents-space' and 'deals-space', in order further to problematize the nature of capitalism and capitalists and explore the ways in which different varieties of capitalists can exert different kinds of influence on political institutions and actors (see Pritchett et al. 2017).

analysis and other new approaches (e.g. NWW 2009) are biased towards elites, in ways that underplay both the role of broader social groups and the role of ideas as well as incentives in shaping the nature of elite behaviour and political settlements more broadly. The third problem lies within the presumption that a given political settlement will tend to have similar effects across different areas of development, despite good evidence that the commitment and capacity of ruling coalitions to deliver development can vary considerably across different domains of development policy.

New theories of limited-access orders and political settlements have so far failed to transcend the lack of sociological depth apparent within 'thin' versions of institutionalist analysis (Portes 2006) and tend to focus on 'inter-elite bargaining' as if this were the only form of state–society relationship that matters. This notion that the politics of development is shaped not only by the configuration of elite power but also by broader state–society relations is emphasized within the comparative historical sociology literature on state-building (e.g. Tilly 1978). For example, work on state-building and development in Southeast Asia by Richard Doner et al. (2005) and Dan Slater (2010) shows how inter-elite bargaining takes place in relation to 'contentious politics' involving popular/subaltern groups expressing their agency and forging various types of alliances with elite groups.[3] The extent to which ruling elites perceive social groups to be a threat to their rule, and/or for their support to be essential for their continuity in power, will shape the nature of their institutional and distributional response to them. Centeno et al.'s reframing (2017) of state capacity and state performance discussed above also makes an important step beyond the 'elitist' focus of the recent turn to politics within international development, to include a focus on how broader social forces shape the capacity of states and commitment of elites to deliver development.[4] As such, the social as well as the political configuration of power within a political settlement plays an influential role in shaping the developmental orientation of ruling coalitions (Kelsall et al. 2022), and will be incorporated in the framework we set out below.

To date, political settlements analysis has tended to draw inspiration from historical and rational actor versions of institutionalist thinking, within

[3] Levi (1988) also seeks to go beyond an elitist focus to emphasize the role of state–society relations in underpinning the fiscal bargain between the state and citizens. The interactions between political institutions, political economy, and organized social groups also follows, in some respects, Atul Kohli's distinction (2004) between 'cohesive capitalist states', 'fragmented multi-class states', and 'neo-patrimonial states'.

[4] They argue, 'the performance of a state cannot be separated from the demands placed on it, the resistance it might meet in accomplishing its goals, and the degree of support or cooperation it enjoys. Hence, states might have had high capacity and leaders may try to deploy it, but outcomes partially rest on how the broader society responds' (Centeno et al. 2017: 12).

which political elites are essentially cast as utility-maximizing rational actors. This offers too narrow a reading of elite political behaviour and motivation (Moe 2005; Levi and Sacks 2009), and ignores the role that ideas as well as incentives play in shaping elite behaviour and the ways that institutions actually function and change over time (Schmidt 2008). As argued by sociological–discursive institutionalists such as Mark Blyth (2010: 99): 'Institutions stabilize the world only because of the constant struggles of agents to impose and contest the ideas that make them possible in the first place.' This is particularly important in terms of the politics of development, with Tuang Vu's seminal analysis (2007) of developmental states in South and Southeast Asia pointing to the significance of the 'roles' that elites perceive that they should be playing, as well as the state capacities they have at their disposal. The challenge here is not to posit ideas as offering an alternative form of motivation but to move beyond the binary established between 'interests' and 'ideas' to explore the ways in which they are intrinsically entwined; as Colin Hay (2011) notes, 'interests' are always perceived and constructed, not objective and given. In the power domains framework that we elaborate below, we incorporate a discursive institutionalist perspective (Schmidt 2008) to help identify the role that ideas play in shaping the politics of development, both within particular political settlements and in relation to specific policy domains.

The third and final challenge flows from this need to go beyond a general-level discussion of how politics shapes elite commitment and state capacity for development, to identify how the politics of development plays out in relation to specific policy challenges. For Merilee Grindle (2017), a characteristic of the new politics and development agenda is the lack of proximity between the level of analysis offered by new accounts of long-run development, on the one hand, and the decision-making realm involving specific development strategies and policies, on the other. This is important if we are interested in helping to explain the capacity and commitment of elites to deliver in relation to different dimensions of development in contemporary settings and to explain why countries often perform unevenly across these different dimensions. As has been argued: 'Detailed historical analyses of the political coalitions and settlements underpinning specific state capacities are essential to increase our understanding of variable state capacity within a polity' (di John and Putzel 2009: 20). In the conceptual framework set out below, we address this by looking beyond the national-level domain of power—or political settlement—to incorporate a focus on a further realm of power—namely, the 'policy domain.'

To recap, new thinking on political settlements constitutes a useful move beyond the limits of new institutionalism, most notably by displacing institutions with power relations as the central focus of analysis. This constitutes the first steps away from what Portes (2006: 238) describes as the 'thin neo-institutionalism' that has beset much political science since the institutional turn in economics took hold, towards a 'thicker' form of institutionalism.[5] However, three further moves are required here, the first two of which involve extending the reach of political settlements analysis to incorporate a focus on the social foundations of power and the role of ideas in shaping political settlements and elite behaviour. The third involves examining how political settlements shape the capacity and commitment to delivering development in relation to *specific* policy domains and challenges. The next section sets out a new conceptual approach—entitled 'power domains'—that seeks to capture these insights within a coherent framework.

Power Domains: Towards a New Conceptual Approach

Building on the insight that theorizing the politics of development needs to start with the configuration of power, rather than institutions per se, our conceptual approach focuses on how the interaction between two key 'power domains' shapes the capacity and commitment to deliver development.[6] The first domain of power involves the general political settlement within a given country, while the second involves specific 'policy domains' (Figure 2.1). Moving beyond the general domain of power to a more specific one reflects the strong likelihood that the politics of securing economic growth, for example, is likely to involve different drivers as compared to the politics of social provisioning (Hickey et al. 2015). This responds to recent calls for the macro-level political analysis of the politics of development to be joined up with more proximate frames of analysis that are better attuned to capturing the politics of reform at lower levels (Grindle 2017). Centeno

[5] Portes (2006: 248) uses the example of privatization in Mexico to show that this profound institutional change became possible only because the president managed to shift the differentials of power that underpinned particular institutional arrangements, in this case through forming an alliance with powerful capitalists and top state bureaucrats. Not for the first time, we are grateful to Matthias vom Hau for drawing our attention to a very useful reference.

[6] We define state capacity as the *ability* of states to apply and implement policy choices within the territorial boundaries they claim to govern. State capacity has internal, external, and territorial components (vom Hau 2012). The internal dimension captures the administrative competence of state agencies involved, such as the expertise and professionalism of their staff. The external component captures proactivity and embeddedness of states in society (Evans 1995). Finally, state capacity also implies territorial reach (O'Donnell 1993; Soifer and vom Hau 2008). Elite commitment can be defined as 'a strong predisposition to a particular course of action that is shared by powerful groups, and which is sustained over time and/or despite obstacles to that course of action' (Chemouni and Hossain 2016).

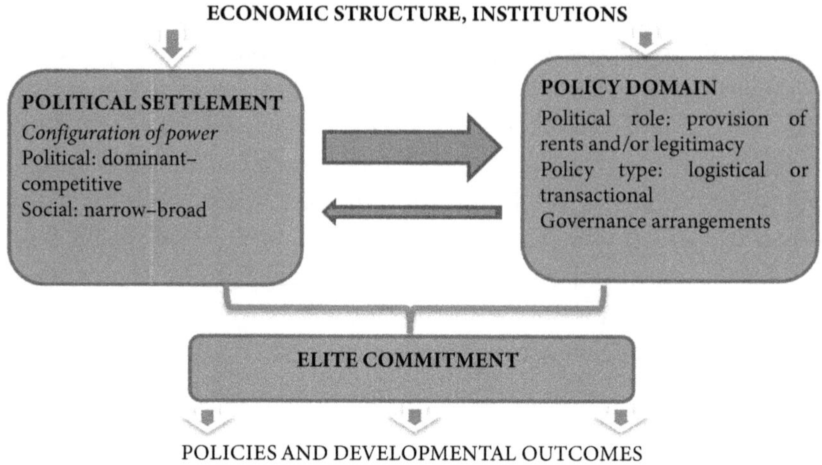

Figure 2.1 Power domains
Source: authors.

et al. (2017) also disaggregate state performance into different dimensions—namely, economic management and inclusion. However, we aim for a higher level of differentiation here, with the notion of policy domains permitting us to examine in more depth the politics of particular realms of development policy that lie within the broader fields of accumulation, redistribution, recognition, and governance (see Chapters 3–6).

As discussed below, our notion of a 'policy *domain*' is intended to denote a more politicized realm than that invoked by the term 'policy *sector*'. It can be defined as a meso-level social field of power relations within which actors promote competing agendas. By arguing that the capacity of states and commitment of elites to deliver particular forms of development is shaped by the interaction of these two overlapping 'power domains'—the political settlement and the policy domain—we join other recent attempts to break from the limitations of institutionalist analysis, and to locate our understanding of institutions within broader fields of power relations (e.g. Goldstone 2004; Sum and Jessop 2013; Fligstein and McAdam 2015). Such approaches may not be amenable to offering up tightly defined variables that can be tested in relation to specific outcomes; however, they do promise to offer more compelling accounts of how different political contexts shape the prospects for development than more parsimonious approaches. The remainder of this section sets out the key characteristics of each of our two main power domains, before turning to the methodological approach that we employed to operationalize the framework in our programme of research into the politics of development.

The Primary Domain of Power: The Political Settlement

The political settlement forms the primary domain of power within our conceptual framework and refers to 'the balance or distribution of power between contending social groups and social classes, on which any state is based' (di John and Putzel 2009: 4). Political settlements are constituted by agreements around the institutional arrangements required to distribute resources and status to powerful organized groups in ways that ensure their acquiescence in maintaining order (Khan 2010). Certain institutional forms will precede and shape political settlements, including those inherited through colonial legacies. However, the ways in which these long-run institutions actually function will be strongly shaped by the configuration of power within a given political settlement at a particular point in time.

Political settlements can be defined by their configuration of power along both political and social dimensions (Kelsall 2018). In political terms we focus on the concentration of power at the apex of government, with regards to the extent to which a ruling coalition faces challenges to its exercise of power and implementation of its policies. If a ruling coalition perceives the threat to its hold on power to be weak, it may feel confident enough to adopt a longer-term horizon towards questions of institution-building and development, with its relative dominance vis-à-vis other elites and organized social groups offering it the capacity to push such reforms through. Where the level of competition for political power is much higher, the threat of losing power means that the incentives for ruling coalitions to use public office and resources to maintain political loyalty through clientelistic means can be overwhelming (Khan 2010, 2017). In such contexts, we may expect to see highly personalized forms of governance and elite capture of institutions and resources, beyond certain 'pockets' of effectiveness that elites may agree must be protected (Levy 2014). The presence of strong excluded coalitions is likely to reduce the time horizons of the ruling coalition and incentivize short-term moves to retain power, whereas being relatively dominant in relation to elites excluded from power may enable ruling coalitions to adopt a longer-time horizon. In theory, then, the highest levels of state capacity for development should be found where ruling coalitions are relatively dominant as opposed to within more competitive settlements.

However, and as indicated above, the configuration of power within a political settlement extends beyond inter-elite relationships to encompass wider forms of state–society relations. The sociological basis of political settlements matters here. This is particularly important in terms of the social groups that ruling coalitions rely on to maintain themselves in power and the extent to which social groups possess the resources and capacities to disrupt the coalition or even the settlement itself. Slater (2010) argues that ruling elites will invest in state-building only when they perceive themselves to be vulnerable to overthrow from below, and therefore seek a means of distributing public goods more broadly to offset this risk because of a perception of 'systemic vulnerability'.

A focus on the social configuration of power also helps to bring into focus the *type* of social groups that ruling coalitions rely on for support and to which they are likely to respond with regards to distributive demands (Kelsall 2018; Kelsall et al. 2022). This is likely to be particularly important when the focus shifts from concerns with economic development to a focus on social or human development. Whereas the early developmental-states literature emphasized the benefits of having a dominant ruling coalition that faced relatively few demands from organized social groups (Leftwich 1994; Evans 1995), the more recent literature on what Patrick Heller and Peter Evans (2010) term 'the Twenty-First Century developmental state' examines the commitment and capacity to deliver human development rather than economic growth per se. From this perspective, it is the strength and nature of the relationships between civil society and political society that count, rather than narrower state-business coalitions. As such, we may expect ruling coalitions that rest on a broad or inclusive configuration of social power to perform better in the realm of social provisioning than those operating on a narrower social basis (Kelsall et al. 2022). In terms of the combinations between different configurations of social and political power, Slater (2010) argues that a dominant ruling coalition that perceives itself to be vulnerable to a systemic threat from mass social groups offers the most conducive combination when it comes to state-building and investments in broad-based development (also Kelsall et al. 2022).

Initial iterations of political settlements analysis tended to emphasize the ways in which different configurations of power generated different types of incentives for ruling elites to respond to. More recently, however, political settlement scholarship has engaged with the role of ideas and ideologies in shaping not just political elite behaviour but political settlements themselves. Ideas are theorized here as constitutive elements of political settlements, being critical to the configuration of power, the perceptions of ruling elites, and their commitment to particular forms of state-building and development (Lavers 2018). Ideas are central to how political settlements function and are maintained, in that these provide 'a relatively coherent set of assumptions about the functioning of economic, social and political institutions' (Béland 2005: 8). These overarching ideas not only shape elite interests, but, as Lavers (2018) notes, 'can also be actively used by actors to achieve their perceived interests, for example, with elites securing the support of lower-level factions through appeals to ideas such as nationalism, social justice or religion'. According to Hazel Gray (2019: 9), 'political commitments to particular political ideologies are a potentially significant force that structures institutions but also the distribution of power', primarily by shaping how legitimate the claims of different groups are perceived to be.

By adopting these insights in our approach, we align with arguments that institutional change is profoundly shaped by ideational factors (Schmidt 2008; Hay 2011). Following earlier work on ideas and institutions by Peter Hall (1993), Vivienne Schmidt's work on 'discursive institutionalism' (2008) engages directly with the significant role played by ideas in shaping politics and processes of reform, not only during periods of institutional crisis (disequilibrium), but also during periods of relative equilibrium. Schmidt identifies three main types of idea: policy ideas that provide potential solutions to predefined social problems; problem definitions that provide ways of framing and understanding particular social issues, in doing so favouring certain types of policy solution and foreclosing the possibility of other types of intervention; and overarching paradigms that serve as road maps, providing 'a relatively coherent set of assumptions about the functioning of economic, social and political institutions' (Schmidt 2008). A further distinction can be made between ideas that are cognitive, which 'elucidate "what is and what to do"', and those that are normative, 'which indicate "what is good or bad about what is" in light of "what one ought to do"' (Schmidt 2008: 306). The relevance of each of these levels and types of ideas for the politics of development is mapped out below (see Figure 2.2). We would locate paradigmatic ideas as operating at the level of the overall political settlement, whereas problem definitions and policy ideas operate primarily in relation to specific policy domains. As our case-study evidence will reveal, in relation to social protection, for example, sustained developmental progress often requires a congruence between ideas across all three levels.

Policy Domain

A 'policy domain' can be defined as a meso-level social field of power relations within which actors promote competing agendas.[7] This more politicized

[7] For other efforts to conceptualize how political settlements and policy domains interact, see Bebbington (2013) and Bebbington et al. (2018) on natural resources, Lavers and Hickey (2016) on social protection, Hickey and Hossain (2019) on education, Nazneen et al. (2019) on women's empowerment, and Pritchett et al. (2017) on growth.

Level of idea	Type of idea	Ideas around development
Paradigm/ philosophy	Normative	How is 'development' understood and who is held responsible for ensuring it? Who deserves development, in what circumstances and on what terms?
	Cognitive	What legitimating ideas enable these normative philosophies to mesh with the programmes and policy ideas below?
Problem definition/ programmes	Normative	What are seen as the main social problems to be solved/goals to be achieved (e.g. poverty reduction, vulnerability, inequality, economic development)? How is this legitimated?
	Cognitive	How are these problems/goals identified? What mechanisms/programmatic responses are considered to be effective in addressing these key problems/goals?
Policy ideas/ solutions	Normative	What ideas are used to legitimate/de-legitimate different policy responses to the above problems? If adopted, how are policies framed?
	Cognitive	Which policy ideas are seen as credible solutions to the above problems? What sources of ideas and evidence are relevant here?

Figure 2.2 The politics of ideas
Source: authors, drawing on Schmidt (2008).

approach to understanding 'sectors' focuses both on the internal characteristics of different domains and on the roles that such domains play in terms of maintaining the political settlement. In particular, what does a particular domain do to help keep political elites in power, whether through the provision of rents and/or popular legitimacy? The nature of this political role is likely to shape the degree of political interference and the relative autonomy that domain-specific actors have within their domain. For example, where an economy is heavily dependent on natural resources, it is likely that ruling elites in clientelist political settlements will seek to play a major role in capturing rents from this domain, with some also using such rents to invest in social provisioning such as cash transfers to maintain popular legitimacy where the social configuration demands this (Mosley 2017). The question is whether the type and level of politicization that occurs has more or fewer developmental consequences: for example, too little politicization can lead to a policy domain becoming marginalized when it comes to budgetary allocations and prioritization regarding implementation, whereas too much can generate problems such as political interference and elite capture.

Specific policy domains are further defined by several internal characteristics, including their governance arrangements, the range of actors and ideas involved in contesting various agendas, the legacies of past policies, and the types of policy challenges involved. Governance arrangements include the processes through which policies are formulated and implemented, and the mechanisms in place to ensure accountability. These processes may be more or less centralized and involve different forms of accountability, but how they actually operate is likely to be less a question of technical design than one of politics. In particular, we would hypothesize that the establishment and nature of such institutional arrangements, and the ways in which they function, are likely to reflect the configuration of power within the broader political settlement (King and Hickey 2017), but also among the particular sets of actors operational within a particular domain.

These arrangements in turn provide the institutional architecture within which different types of actors manoeuvre and seek to exert their influence within the domain. The key actors will differ by domain, and are likely to include a mixture of politicians and bureaucrats at multiple levels, private-sector actors (firms and individual capitalists), civil-society actors (e.g. unions, business associations, advocacy organizations, movements), development agencies, and other ‘politically salient stakeholders’ (Levy and Walton 2013). The incentives and ideas of these actors, and their capacity to form coalitions across different interest groups and around particular ideas (Leftwich 2010), will closely shape the possibilities for different types of reforms to emerge and gain priority within a given domain. The types of ideas that seem to matter most within policy domains are problem definitions and policy solutions (Figure 2.2), where the mobilization of evidence (cognitive ideas) may be influential in shaping policy responses.

The political settlement and policy domain relate closely to each other along this ideational dimension: it is likely that those policy actors and entrepreneurs promoting particular policy ideas within specific domains will need to frame these in ways that fit with overarching elite paradigms.

The types of policy challenge that characterize different policy domains, or dimensions thereof, can have significant implications for how the politics of development plays out in practice. One distinction to be drawn here is between policy challenges that are primarily 'logistical' in nature, whereby the problem is largely one that can be solved through technical means (e.g. employing more staff, delivering more resources, building more infrastructure); and challenges that are 'transactional', which may require shifts in behaviour and multiple forms of human interaction at multiple levels before progress can occur (Andrews et al. 2012). An example of a logistical challenge might be building more schools to enable greater access in remote rural areas. On the other hand, ensuring that teachers are trained to a high level, remain on task, and help improve learning outcomes constitutes a more transactional challenge. Meeting these different types of policy challenge requires different types of governance capacity and, our conceptual framework would suggest, the support and agency of different types of coalition.

The main contention that flows from the 'power domains' framework set out here, then, is that the interaction between particular types of political settlement and particular policy domains will shape the capacity and commitment of elites to deliver specific forms of development. Although this may be shaped by historical legacies and existing endowments, such 'initial conditions' are not prescriptive and may be navigated and deployed in very different ways depending on how coalitions are able to navigate the specific configurations of power they find themselves within.

Methodological Approach and Country Cases

> Research into how institutions are formed, sustained and changed requires detailed historical, comparative and theoretical enquiry, drawing on a wide range of disciplinary perspectives in which questions are asked not only about structures, but also about agents, leadership and ideas in politics.
>
> **(Leftwich 2005: 596)**

In applying our framework, we followed a comparative approach whereby country cases were chosen based on their representation of different types of political settlements. We focused in particular on four of the 'most likely' cases to exemplify the given types, with Ghana and Bangladesh often portrayed as archetypal forms of competitive settlements, for example, and Rwanda as a dominant type, but we were also alert to the transitions that some cases seemed to be going through along the dominant–competitive axis, as with previously dominant Uganda becoming subject to higher levels of competitive pressures over time. Investigations were then conducted within several different policy domains in each context to enable both cross- and within-case comparisons; this always involved our four main case-study countries, but in some policy domains our research was extended to a broader range of cases, each of which was again chosen because of the particular type of political settlement it represented. For example, our work on both social assistance and pockets of bureaucratic effectiveness included Kenya and Zambia; on economic growth, we had a sample of ten countries that included two from Southeast Asia; our work on gender equity looked at anti-domestic violence legislation in India and South Africa; and, on education, we included Cambodia as well as South Africa. Appendix II offers a brief introduction to the main country contexts in which we worked.

Our selection of policy domains—namely, economic growth, natural-resource governance, women's interests, social assistance, education, health, and governance—was based on several criteria. The first was that they should be of significance to the development trajectory of a wide range of countries and to the well-being of citizens therein. The second was that they should offer insights into different types of policy domain, some of which were closely associated with the perils of rent-seeking such as oil governance, while others seemed more closely related to issues of legitimacy such as education. This was to gain traction on the different roles that different policy domains play in maintaining political order and regime continuity. The third was to include a focus on different kinds of policy challenge, including challenges that are largely logistical in nature (e.g. delivering cash transfers) and those that are more transactional (e.g. raising the quality of learning in schools). The final and cross-cutting challenge was to identify domains that presented puzzles for which other conceptual approaches had struggled to provide compelling explanations. For example, institutionalist accounts of the resource curse have come under increasing criticism, with some advocating for a political settlements-type analysis to generate stronger insights (Poteete 2009). In terms of social assistance, our initial effort to map progress against typical development indicators—namely, economic growth and levels of democracy—generated little observable pattern and indicated the need to look for more contextually grounded explanations. On education, the problem of learning had simply not been subject to political analysis, with most existing work focusing on the quantity rather than the quality of education. And so on. In each case, then, there was a puzzle that lay at least partially unanswered by mainstream analysis.

According to George and Bennett (2005: 149), this form of 'typological theorizing, which combines methods of both cross-case comparisons and process-tracing, is a powerful way to create middle-range theories that are consistent with both the historical explanations of individual cases and the general theoretical patterns evident across such cases'. Importantly for our concerns, this type of approach promises to produce more policy-relevant forms of analysis, by seeking to identify the extent to which particular reforms or interventions play out in similar ways across similar types of political settlement.[8] Within each comparative study of a particular domain, the usual approach was to identify an outcome variable across each case and then use process-tracing to try and track this back to the underlying political conditions within each case. The key outcomes that we examined were the levels of elite commitment to delivering a particular outcome and the capacity of the ruling coalition to deliver on this. In terms of analysis, each case was subjected to within-case analysis before cross-case comparative analysis was undertaken. For this book (Chapter 7), we have extended our comparative analysis to stretch across domains as well as cases.

[8] For George and Bennett (2005: 7), 'typological theories can guide researchers towards questions and research designs whose results will be pertinent to problems faced by policymakers. One of the chief goals of political science ... is to provide policymakers with "generic knowledge" that can help them form effective strategies'; and for Bennett (2003: 5, cited in George and Bennett 2005: 7), 'such differentiated theories not only allow for more discriminating explanations; they are also of greater practical value for policymakers, who can use them to make more discriminating diagnoses of emerging situations'.

3

Political Economy Puzzles

How Do Countries Grow and How Can They Avoid the Natural-Resource Curse?

Economic development—by which we mean broad-based economic growth with rapid structural transformation—is important, and not only because it enables widespread improvements in living standards. For Khan (2010), structural transformation that is sustained over time can lead to a transition from a clientelist to a capitalist political settlement, within which informal and highly personalized institutions (or 'deals') are increasingly displaced by the formal and impersonal institutions (or 'rules') associated with Weberian forms of governance.[1] Historically, a prerequisite for successful economic development has been an effective state (Kohli 2004). The emergence of effective states in developing countries is

> best thought of as the product of the way in which the political processes operate together, dynamically, to forge fundamental rules and agreements (and ensure compliance with them) about the use and distribution of power and the political practices which are the necessary basis for the establishment and maintenance of public institutions.
>
> **(Leftwich 2007: 11)**

Understanding why countries differ in their economic development paths needs a framework of analysis that recognizes the centrality of power and politics.

The original developmental states of East Asia had one unifying economic characteristic: they witnessed almost uninterrupted rapid economic growth for well over four decades during the second half of the twentieth century. This is very different from what we have observed in other developing countries, where economic growth has generally been boom and bust

[1] This occurs because the growth of the formal economy offers governments sufficient revenue to redistribute through official mechanisms (thus reducing their reliance on rent-generating and rent-seeking activities) and because the emergence of more autonomous forms of capitalist firms reduces rent-seeking behaviour by market actors (Khan 2010).

Pathways to Development. Sam Hickey and Kunal Sen, Oxford University Press.
 DOI: 10.1093/oso/9780198872566.003.0003

(Kar et al. 2013), defined by a rapid growth acceleration followed by a deceleration that at times was quite prolonged. In our research on economic growth, we sought to address the puzzle of why developing countries have rarely witnessed sustained economic growth, as well as why rapid accelerations in economic growth have been possible in weak institutional contexts. Part of the puzzle regarding the patterns of economic growth witnessed in developing countries over the late twentieth and early twenty first century, including the difficulties of moving from growth to structural transformation, relates to the dependence of many economies in the global south on natural resources. With the commodity super-cycle of the early twenty-first century helping to accelerate the discovery of commercial quantities of both hydrocarbons and minerals in many developing countries, the promise of newfound natural-resource wealth became widespread in many countries, particularly those within the Gulf of Guinea and throughout East Africa. That many such finds were in countries with weak governance contexts raised concerns that the 'resource curse' would come to afflict an even wider range of countries, unless they could forge accountable and transparent institutional arrangements for managing natural resources. In this chapter we examine the tricky questions of how to maintain economic growth and of avoiding the resource curse in turn, in order to assess the extent to which a power domains approach can help offer some hitherto missing parts of each of these puzzles.

How Do Countries Grow?

The usual definition of economic growth holds that it is a sustained increase in per capita incomes over a sufficiently long period (see Spence 2008).[2] Much of the academic and policy literature on economic growth has focused on the determinants of long-run economic growth across countries. However, the focus on long-run economic growth misses the point that most countries observe dramatic fluctuations in growth of per capita income (Sen 2013). Very few developing countries meet the criterion of sustained high rates of economic growth; rather, most tend to observe stop–go growth episodes, with growth accelerations followed by growth decelerations or collapses. As Jones and Olken (2008: 582) point out:

> almost all countries in the world have experienced rapid economic growth lasting a decade or longer, during which they converge towards income levels in

[2] This section draws on a comparative project coordinated by Kunal Sen and Lant Pritchett, the fuller results of which are presented in Pritchett et al. (2017).

> the United States. Conversely, nearly all countries have experienced periods of abysmal growth. Circumstances or policies that produce ten years of rapid economic growth appear easily reversed, often leaving countries no better off than they were prior to the expansion.

This suggests that economic growth in developing countries is *episodic*—massive discrete *changes* in growth are common, with most developing countries experiencing distinct growth *episodes* and growth accelerations and decelerations or collapses as transitions between those episodes (Pritchett et al. 2016, 2017). If economic growth patterns in most developing countries are mostly episodic and rarely stable, this suggests that influential explanations of the drivers of economic development that stress the primacy of inclusive economic and political institutions (e.g. Acemoglu and Robinson 2012) are not able to explain why growth accelerates in a particular country, followed often by a deceleration. A credible account of the politics of economic growth should be able to differentiate between political and institutional factors that can cause economic growth to accelerate after a period of prolonged stagnation or collapse, and those that can explain why growth, once initiated, is sometimes maintained but, more often than not, rarely sustained.

From a power domains approach, we set out to explore Khan's proposition that the nature of ruling coalitions within specific types of political settlement would exert a powerful influence over the extent to which ruling elites would invest in growth-enhancing institutions. Going further to explore the policy domain around economic accumulation, we devised two main analytical tools to understand domain-level governance arrangements therein, namely, the 'deals space' and the 'rents space'. The 'deals space' is the set of personalized and informal relationships between political elites and economic actors (Figure 3.1). The 'rents space' is the rent extraction possibilities from different sectors of the economy, with rent-thick sectors, such as mining, utilities, and telecommunications, having a different implication for economic growth dynamics, as compared to more competitive sectors, such as export-orientated manufacturing and the informal sector (Figure 3.2). Both tools yielded important insights into the nature of state–business relations in the country in question, which went beyond the limits of characterizing state–business relations as being either wholly collusive or wholly synergistic, based on an aggregate profile. In our case studies, the nature of deals differed across sectors, with deals being offered to firms in a sector depending on the holding power of the firms and how elites viewed the sector within the prevailing political settlement. Closed ordered deals—that

	Closed	Open
	(deals are available only to specific individuals/organization)	(deals depend on actions of agents, but not identities)
Ordered (once negotiated, deals will be honoured)	Only those with political connections get to make deals, but they can be confident that officials will deliver	Anyone can make a deal, and they can be certain that officials will deliver
Disordered (deals will not be honoured)	Only those with political connections get to make deals, and even they cannot be certain that officials will deliver	Anyone can make a deal, but no one is certain that officials will deliver

Figure 3.1 The deals space
Source: Pritchett, Sen, and Werker (2017).

	Rent-thick sectors	Competitive sectors
Export-oriented	Natural resources (rentiers)	Export-oriented manufacturing (magicians)
Domestic market	Utilities, finance, telecommunications (powerbrokers)	Subsistence agriculture, informal sector in manufacturing and services (workhorses)

Figure 3.2 The rents space
Source: Pritchett, Sen, and Werker (2017).

is, deals that, once made, were likely to be honoured by the political elite, and offered only to those with political connections—were more likely if the sector was a mechanism of rent extraction, while open deals—those that were offered to a wider set of economic actors—were more likely if the sector was politically salient in the economic growth process. In general, firms in rent-thick sectors made different demands of the state as compared to firms in more competitive sectors, with firms in rent-thick sectors preferring weak state capacity to regulate and enforce. This implied that, where firms in rent-thick sectors were politically important, weak state capacity around industrial policy was likely to occur, with detrimental effects on structural transformation. The absence of firms in export-orientated manufacturing sectors in some country contexts implied that there was little pressure on ruling elites to build better state capacity for effective industrial policy, making it more difficult for the economy to diversify away from commodity exports.

In our framework, economic growth and the degree to which that growth is characterized by structural transformation is an outcome of the nature of deals offered to economic actors. This in turn is a function of the political settlement and the rents space (Pritchett et al. 2017). Economic growth episodes then influence the political settlement and the rents space by positive or negative feedback loops, which in turn impact on the deals space, affecting future growth.

We used our framework to address two questions: (*i*) why does economic growth accelerate under certain political conditions and not in others? And (*ii*) why is it difficult to maintain economic growth over a long period? We summarize our findings to these two questions, drawing specifically from the experiences of ten countries in Africa and Asia.

What Ignites Economic Growth?

According to our framework, economic growth is likely to accelerate when there is a movement in the deals space from disordered to ordered deals. Ordered deals mean that an investor's time horizon for realizing returns is lengthened, which makes a greater set of investments profitable over the long term. There may be an additional quid pro quo in which ordered deals allow the state to ask investors to commit to the investment decision and engage in production, so that rents can be generated through the production process. This commitment to ordered deals needs to be seen as credible by investors: they must believe that the state or its agents will not renege on its implicit or explicit promise not to expropriate future rents, especially after investment decisions involving sunk costs in fixed capital have been taken (Sen 2013).

A commitment to 'ordered deals' is more likely in dominant political settlements, where a strong political leadership allows for the likelihood of deals, once negotiated, to be honoured (ordered deals) and of credible commitment by elites to economic growth. The economic growth accelerations that occur during such political settlements may arise in rentier or powerbroker quadrants and may support an ever-more-exclusive political elite whose power comes from patronage or repression. To contrast with dominant party settlements, the cycling of factions in and out of power in competitive clientelist settlements leads to shorter political time horizons, which undermines the potential for ordered deals to emerge.

For example, economic growth accelerated in 1983 in Ghana, with the taking of executive power after a coup by General Jerry Rawlings; in 1994 in Rwanda, with the coming to power of the dominant Rwandan Patriotic Front (RPF); and in 1988 in Uganda, within two years of National Resistance Movement (NRM) taking power; these often led to closed ordered deals that catalysed rapid increases in incomes within a short time (Pritchett et al. 2017). In each case, the new ruling coalition was able to impose order and see through difficult reforms, having established a degree of dominance over excluded elite factions through a mixture of repression, co-optation, and an inclusive discourse of nation-building. Further, the ideology of the ruling coalition mattered in shaping the commitment of political elites to an economic growth-orientated strategy that privileged ordered deal-making over short-term populism and disordered deals. The pro-growth ideology of the ruling coalitions in Rwanda and Uganda was itself in part shaped by the economic collapse and unstable political settlements associated with periods of conflict prior to the emergence of these coalitions. Ruling elites in these countries viewed an economic growth-orientated strategy as a mechanism to legitimize the regime and prevent a return to political instability and economic chaos.

In Uganda, after coming to power in 1986, President Museveni moved quickly to form a broad-based ruling coalition that led to political stability and a conducive environment for ordered deals (Bukenya and Hickey 2019). Further reforms from 1987 onwards—such as the process of privatization that was used as a mechanism of rent-sharing with powerful elites and the return of property to Asian businesspeople in return for political loyalty and financial support—also bolstered the capacity of the ruling coalition to be in power, contributing to the maintenance of an ordered deals environment. Importantly, the president also invested, with international support, in building the capacity of the economic technocracy to impose fiscal discipline and macroeconomic stability (see Chapter 6 for more on these 'pockets of effectiveness'). As a result, Uganda witnessed one of Africa's most successful episodes of economic recovery and sustained economic growth.

Not all economic growth accelerations occurred in dominant party settlements—one of the largest accelerations in economic growth (measured by Net Present Value of the cumulative change in GDP per capita) occurred in India in 1993 after four decades of economic stagnation, when India had already moved decisively from a strong dominant party (under the Congress from independence till the early 1980s) to a competitive clientelist political settlement. The shift from an anti-business to a pro-business ideology among ruling elites from the mid-1980s led to an ordering of deals from the late 1980s onwards, with the pro-business ideology broadly shared among two major political parties, Congress and the Bharatiya Janata Party (BJP), which meant that a commitment to economic growth-orientated policies remained in place irrespective of the election results. A similar phenomenon was observed in Bangladesh, where the two parties that alternated in power (the Awami League and the Bangladesh National Party (BNP)) shared a commitment to ordered deals for the major economic growth sectors in the economy (such as ready-made garments). Here, ordered deals were maintained to 'magicians'—exporters in competitive sectors—through a process of rent-sharing across the political divide, no matter which political party was in power. In Liberia, an economic growth acceleration occurred from the mid-2000s, as regional powers, backed by the United States and the international financial institutions and buoyed by favourable commodity prices, brokered and enforced a peace that ended some three decades of instability, war, and economic decline. This shows the potential of external actors to reverse home-grown negative feedback loops, even in a competitive clientelist settlement.

Why Is Economic Growth Difficult to Maintain?

The subsequent evolution of the political settlement and the limited political power of firms in competitive sectors (such as export-orientated manufacturing) was important in explaining the extent of structural transformation of the economy and the maintenance of economic growth. However, a positive economic growth episode underpinned by a closed ordered deals environment (often in dominant party settings) became increasingly vulnerable to challenges from non-elites as well as excluded elites, and political delegitimation of the growth process. This led to the increasing possibility of the deals environment becoming disordered, and acted as a constraint to structural transformation and for economic growth to be 'locked in'. An example of such an unravelling of a closed ordered deals environment leading to a deceleration in economic growth was evident in India, when the 'crony capitalism' tendencies associated with the rapid growth acceleration in the early 2000s led to pushback from third-party enforcement institutions, such as the judiciary and the audit authorities, and to political mobilization of non-elites, leading to a shift to disordered deals and a deceleration in economic growth.

Thus, the changing balance of power between different groups was in part shaped by the composition of economic growth within a given economy, according a relative and changing degree of influence on capitalists in different sectors. This balance of power helped shift the allocation of resources and opportunities, both within and between different kinds of capitalists, in ways that then had feedback effects regarding the nature of the deals space. For example, increased reliance on monopolistic and rentier forms of capitalism may have had positive effects in terms of aggregate economic growth levels, but this tended to produce negative feedback effects, both on the nature of the deals space (which could move from being relatively open to more closed) and on overall rates of structural transformation.[3] This suggested a trade-off, whereby having GDP growth today can store up institutional problems for tomorrow if it is in the 'wrong' sectors.

None of our main case-study countries—Bangladesh, Ghana, Rwanda, and Uganda—showed rapid uninterrupted economic growth accompanied by robust structural transformation and a move from closed to open deals (much less credibly institutionalized rules). In the case of Bangladesh and Ghana, this was principally due to the nature of the political settlement, where competitive clientelism did not allow political and bureaucratic elites the long-time horizon necessary to build long-term productive capacity in the more dynamic economic growth sectors, diversifying economic activity from low value-added labour-intensive goods, in the case of Bangladesh, and primary commodities in Ghana. In the case of Rwanda and Uganda, where the dominant nature of the political settlement allowed elites to maintain closed ordered deals for segments of a sector where they saw a strategic interest (as in the case of oil in Uganda, discussed below, and coffee in Rwanda), the lack of organizational power of economic elites operating in the more dynamic sectors meant that there was not sufficient interest among political elites in generating the collective capacity and commitment required for a move

[3] For example, the prolonged economic growth acceleration in Ghana since 1983 has not been accompanied by structural transformation and a move to open ordered deals, mainly due to the limited political power of the magicians (export-orientated manufacturing) relative to the rentiers and powerbrokers (Pritchett et al. 2017). As we discuss later in this chapter, the deals environment around natural-resource governance has progressively worsened in the country since the major oil find of 2006.

towards structural transformation (Pritchett et al. 2017). There is also the sense that that, as elsewhere in East Africa (Gray 2018), 'dominant' presidents have been fearful of supporting the development of a strong domestic capitalist class, given the potential political threat that wealthy and autonomous capitalists might pose to their political survival in contexts where political opposition is otherwise largely nullified.

The experiences of Malaysia and Thailand is particularly revealing in showing how rapid economic growth was difficult to maintain (Sen and Tyce 2018). These two countries had economic growth acceleration episodes with rapid growth for over three decades from the 1950s to the late 1990s accompanied by structural transformation. However, economic growth decelerated following the 1997 Asian financial crisis (AFC) and has not recovered to its previous rapid levels in the twenty years since the onset of this crisis.

The economic growth acceleration phases in Malaysia and Thailand were characterized by political elites in these two countries following dualistic deals where they offered open ordered deals to *magicians*—that is, firms in the export-orientated manufacturing sector—and, at the same time, offered closed ordered deals to *powerbrokers*—mostly domestic firms operating in non-tradable sectors or in manufacturing sectors that were protected to a large extent from foreign competition—and, in the case of Malaysia, also to *rentiers*. In the case of Malaysia, the dualistic deals environment was an outcome of the *strong dominant party* political settlement, which attempted to balance the need for political stability (through rents that were created for powerful Malay groups in the society via the closed deals with powerbrokers) with the need for high rates of economic growth that occurred from the open ordered deals offered to magicians. In the case of Thailand, the dualistic deals environment was more a result of a shift to a *competitive clientelist* political settlement in the 1970s, as well as the means of securing the support of the military and monarchy to the economic growth strategy followed by Thai political elites.

The dualistic deals environments served Malaysia and Thailand well in the first economic growth phase, as high growth and fast rates of structural transformation ensued with the rapid expansion of the export-orientated manufacturing sector. However, towards the mid-1990s, negative feedback loops were observed in both countries, with the political settlement in Malaysia moving from *strong dominant party* to a *vulnerable authoritarian* political settlement after the AFC, and the *competitive–clientelist* political settlement in Thailand shifting to a *vulnerable authoritarian* political settlement by the 2000s. In the case of Malaysia, the closed ordered deals that were offered to Malay entrepreneurs, as a means of countering the power of Malaysia's

Chinese capitalist class, had largely failed to create a dynamic Malay capitalist class that could compete effectively in world markets, and led to a dualistic industrial structure, with multinationals operating in the export-orientated manufacturing sector and globally uncompetitive Malay conglomerates in the domestically orientated manufacturing and service sectors. In the case of Thailand, local content requirements in the automobiles and electronics sectors had created a large number of Thai companies, which successfully became supplier firms to the multinationals operating in these sectors. As a consequence, Thailand observed higher rates of structural transformation than Malaysia in their respective economic growth deceleration episodes, though not at the same pace as in the pre-AFC phase. In both countries, the dualistic deals environments had become increasingly patronage based and increasingly disordered after the AFC and, as a consequence, limited the possibility of high economic growth returning to Malaysia and Thailand after the economic downturn caused by the AFC.

Therefore, while dualistic deals strategies in Malaysia and Thailand *could and did* deliver economic growth for quite a long while, these strategies had their 'sell-by date'. In both these countries, the clientelist nature of the prevailing political settlement, even with impressive levels of structural transformation (as compared to other developing countries), acted as a constraining factor in the transition from deals capitalism to rules capitalism. Open ordered deals in the magician space could not compensate indefinitely for a lack of policy coherence and open order provided to workhorse firms as well as the negative spillover effects originating from the closed deals offered to rentiers and powerbrokers.

As suggested by our framework, the interaction of the political settlement with the rents space determined in large part the deals that were offered to economic actors by political/economic elites. The nature of deals—whether they were closed or open, disordered or ordered—then explained whether economic growth accelerated from a period of stagnation or collapse, and whether growth was maintained. We find in our country case studies that the nature of deals differed across sectors, with deals being offered to firms in a sector depending on the political power of the firms in the sector, and how elites viewed the sector within the prevailing political settlement. Closed ordered deals were likely to be offered to firms in the sector if the sector was a mechanism of rent extraction or creation (typically, these were rentier and powerbroker sectors), with open deals more likely if the sector was politically salient in the economic growth process (typically, these were magician sectors). Our approach to the political economy of economic growth showed the importance of moving beyond a focus on the institutional and political determinants of long-run growth (as in the work of NWW 2009 and Acemoglu and Robinson 2012), to an understanding of why most developing countries see moves back and forth in economic as well as institutional development.

Three policy implications follow from our findings. First, wholesale reforms that aim to improve the national 'investment climate' or aim to create a 'level playing field' are unlikely to work in deals-based economies. There is huge variation in the deals environment for firms within the same country, which suggests that, instead of just looking at the overall national investment 'climate', we should look at how micro-climates for different kinds of firms are created and to what extent they can enable ordered deals to happen. For the policymaker, it may be better to concentrate on initiatives that may have minimal impact on *de jure* policy but that signal a decisive shift in policy implementation. Such a shift may have substantial impacts on investor expectations and initiate an acceleration of economic growth.

Secondly, while conventional approaches to industrial policy highlight the importance of selective intervention on the part of the state to promote high-productivity firms and industries (or industries with the maximum learning by doing effects; see Aiginger and Rodrik 2020), our findings also suggest that discretionary industrial policy risks being used for rent-seeking purposes and directly unproductive activities. The challenge for policymakers is to devise 'institutionally robust' industrial policies when state capacity for implementation and regulation is low, especially in aid- and resource-dependent countries, where rentier and powerbroker firms may have a significant political voice.

Finally, for economic growth to be maintained, it is necessary for policymakers to create the conditions for magician and workhorse firms to exist and flourish, as the political demands of these firms would improve the country's overall chance at success and structural transformation. In addition, the capability of the economic bureaucracy needs to be strengthened so that they are capable of offering open ordered deals to magician and workhorse firms and are insulated from the demands of rentier and powerbroker firms for closed deals.

How Can Countries Avoid the Natural-resource Curse?

The commodity super-cycle of the early twenty-first century coincided with the discovery of commercial quantities of both hydrocarbons and minerals in many developing countries, including around the Gulf of Guinea and in

East Africa.[4] The fact that many such finds were in countries with weak governance contexts raised concerns that the 'resource curse' would come to afflict an even wider range of countries unless they could forge accountable and transparent institutional arrangements for managing natural resources. In this section we use a two-country comparison of new producers in Africa to examine the tricky question of why some countries work harder to avoid the resource curse than others by deploying a power domains approach as an alternative to the usual institutionalist analysis used to explore this puzzle.

By the early 2000s, it had become an article of faith that countries can avoid the so-called resource curse only if they have the right institutions in place at the moment when commercial quantities of natural resources are discovered.[5] Influenced by neo-institutionalist economics and the experience of well-governed oil-rich countries like Norway, this perspective has led international agencies to promote a remarkably similar range of reforms in Africa. This includes a separation of regulatory and commercial activities, mechanisms to ensure transparency and accountability at each stage of the value chain, and institutions to offset dangers of Dutch Disease (e.g. sovereign wealth funds).

However, a growing amount of evidence suggests that institutions may be of secondary importance to the good governance of natural resources as compared to the role played by ruling coalitions (Poteete 2009), and that adopting best-practice legislation may be ineffective in developing countries (Thurber et al. 2011). This critique fits with the broader move away from the tendency to support western-style institutional arrangements via the 'good-governance' agenda, given the extent to which the same arrangements can have very different effects in different political conditions (Rodrik 2004); the distortions and costs that such processes of 'isomorphic mimicry' can entail, including the loss of existing state capabilities (Andrews et al. 2012); and the likelihood that, where reforms do not fit with the incentives of ruling elites, they will probably be subject to being either ignored or captured for other purposes (Khan 2005).

[4] This section draws on a comparative project coordinated by Sam Hickey, with case-study research led by Kojo Asante, Abdul-Gafaru-Abdulai, and Giles Mohan in Ghana and by Angelo Izama and Sam Hickey in Uganda. Fuller results can be found in Hickey and Izama (2016, 2020), Mohan et al. (2018), and Hickey et al. (2020)

[5] e.g. Humphreys et al. 2007; NRGI 2014. See Thurber et al. 2011 for a powerful critique of this approach.

Our Research Design

To test the relative accuracy of these two alternative readings—one derived from new institutionalism the other from political settlements analysis—we chose two newly oil-rich countries that had broadly comparable oil finds, but that differed significantly in terms of both their institutional arrangements and the nature of their political settlements—namely, Ghana and Uganda. Both countries identified commercial quantities of oil at around the same time and at a similar level of economic value, both in absolute terms and as a proportion of contribution to gross domestic product (see Table 2.1). Ghana's estimated proven reserves are small when compared to oil discoveries in other countries in Africa, such as Angola and Nigeria. The Jubilee oilfield was developed in a record time of three years and commenced production in November 2010. Ghana's total oil reserves are expected to increase, plus associated natural gas. With up to 6.5 billion barrels of oil reserves in the western part of the country, of which between 1.4 and 1.7 billion barrels are probably recoverable, Uganda sits in the mid-range of Africa's oil-owning countries (Patey 2017). However, and despite entering a joint venture partnership with three international oil companies (IOCs) in 2014, production has been heavily delayed amid falling oil prices, strong disagreements between the Government of Uganda (GoU) and IOCs and also a limited degree of cooperation among IOCs themselves.[6] In the study reported here, and to control for the fact that Ghana has already moved into production, whereas Uganda's deposits have yet to do so, we focus our comparison only on those upstream aspects of oil governance that each country engaged with over the same historical period—that is, 2006–14.

The more significant differences concern their respective levels of development and governance: according to standard measures, Ghana far outstrips Uganda along virtually every dimension (see Table 3.1).[7] Ghana not only records much higher levels of per capita income and human development; it is also judged to be more democratic and more effectively governed than Uganda, which exhibits higher levels of corruption and authoritarian tendencies. From a good governance perspective, then, there would be strong expectations that Ghana would be in a better position to govern its oil more effectively than Uganda (Table 3.2).

[6] The ongoing negotiations between GoU and the IOCs are dealt with in (Hickey and Izama 2020).

[7] We present data here as close as possible to the point of oil discovery. Polity IV operates on a scale of −10 to +10, while the World Governance Indicators use a scale of −2.5 to +2.5.

Table 3.1 Oil in Ghana and Uganda compared

Comparative dimensions	Ghana	Uganda
Major discovery	2007 (offshore)	2006 (onshore)
Production begins	November 2010	2023 (est.)
Projected lifespan	*c.*2030	*c.*2040
Volume (recoverable)	2bn+ barrels	1–1.4bn barrels
Economic value	3–4% GDP	4–5% GDP pa

Source: authors.

Table 3.2 Comparing Ghana and Uganda through a 'good-governance' lens

Comparative dimensions	Ghana	Uganda
Development indicators	$1,570 GDP per capita 135/187 HDI (medium) Economic growth: 5.6% (2001–10)	$500 GDP per capita 161/187 HDI (low) Economic growth: 7–8% (2001–10)
Democracy (data from Polity IV 2010)	Multi-party since 1992 Democratic: 8 Polity IV	Multi-party since 2005 Closed anocracy: −1 Polity IV
Governance indicators (WGI 2006)	Voice and accountability: 0.37 Govt effectiveness: 0.11 Rule of law: 0.00 Control of corruption: 0.02	Voice and accountability: −0.42 Govt effectiveness: −0.48 Rule of law: −0.34 Control of corruption: −0.75

Source: authors.

However, from a political settlements perspective, we might hypothesize that Uganda's 'dominant' ruling coalition may be inclined to take a longer-term view of oil governance than Ghana's, which finds itself subject to intense electoral pressures and a need to secure quick wins.

As discussed earlier, Ghana has since the early 1990s been characterized by a high degree of competition between elite factions that formed around two main political parties. Tightly fought elections and relatively frequent turnovers mean that ruling coalitions are continually in a vulnerable position vis-à-vis alternative coalitions with the capacity to wrest power from them. Meanwhile, the advent of oil appears to have further intensified inter-elite competition for power (Whitfield et al. 2015; Mohan et al. 2018), threatening a vicious rather than virtual spiral with regards to the expected relationships between political competition and institutional development. Uganda, meanwhile, represents a 'dominant' form of political settlement, whereby the ruling coalition has ensured its longevity by actively seeking to co-opt and/or repress rival elite actors and factions. The current president has been in power since 1986, and, while there has been little sign of a sustained state-building project, some effort has been made to protect certain bureaucratic enclaves within economic governance from political interference in ways that have had developmental outcomes (Whitfield et al. 2015).

To explore this, we focused on two main aspects of governance within the domain of oil: the deal-making process with international oil companies, within which we focused on how far governments were willing and able to secure relatively high rates of return for their treasuries vis-à-vis what IOCs would take; and the process through which new institutional arrangements were put in place to govern oil, and the extent to which they were enforced.

Methodologically, we undertook over sixty interviews with key stakeholders in each country between 2013 and 2015; wherever possible, we used documentary and statistical evidence from other sources to triangulate with our interview data, such as comparative reports on the share taken by African governments in comparable deal-making processes. However, the qualitative method was the only viable means of getting inside the 'black box' of policy- and deal-making within the notoriously secretive world of oil governance. The fact that we were able to interview officials from government and oil companies who were directly involved in the oil negotiations, as well as close observers of these processes from parliaments and civil society, further enhances the reliability and (internal) validity of the evidence presented here.

Oil Governance under Different Political Settlements: Ghana and Uganda Compared

The results confirmed a 'power domains' reading of oil governance, particularly in terms of the influence that different types of political settlements can have over governance. Ghana moved from discovery in 2007 to production in 2010 in record-breaking speed. The initial impetus came from the then ruling New Patriotic Party (NPP) government ahead of the 2008 elections, with oil-company officials reporting that they were pushed by government to implement a '"quick and dirty" plan that would cut corners to exploit the field as quickly as possible' (Gary 2009: 24). The new National Democratic Congress (NDC) government that took office in January 2009 maintained this accelerated pace. Officials working within Ghana's National Petroleum Corporation told us that the NDC was determined to ensure that oil revenues were on the books before the 2012 elections to help secure them a second term. Despite being urged to adopt new institutional arrangements for governing oil, in line with the Norway model, this meant that Ghana made deals with oil companies in an unregulated environment and without addressing what external observers had identified as a chronic lack of bureaucratic and technical capacity along the whole oil value chain (World Bank 2009). When the new arrangements for governing oil were eventually established in 2014, they were lauded by observers as reflecting international best practice, including safeguards against 'Dutch Disease' effects, such as provisions that prevented governments from borrowing against future oil earnings. However, keen to collateralize debt to help secure a large infrastructure loan from China, the NDC government whipped its politicians to overturn this regulation. The acceptance of the $3 billion loan was among several politically driven examples of macroeconomic mismanagement that helped drive up Ghana's debt ratio to such levels that an International Monetary Fund (IMF) austerity programme was re-established in 2015. Within a decade of discovering commercial quantities of oil, Ghana's polity and economy was exhibiting signs of having succumbed to elements of the resource curse (Fosu 2017), from deepened levels of clientelist politics (Whitfield et al. 2015; Mohan et al. 2018) through to weakened economic performance (Osei et al. 2017).

In Uganda, meanwhile, deal-making with IOCs was halted until new legislative arrangements were put in place in 2013, with the government keen to devise instruments such as Production Sharing Agreements that could underpin a strong bargaining position. The process through which new institutional arrangements were pushed into legislation was in most respects less democratic than in Ghana, with the president going to great lengths to ensure that strong executive control over the sector was inscribed in the new laws. However, there was significant opposition from parliamentarians, including many from the ruling party who formed a cross-party alliance, Parliamentary Forum on Oil and Gas, to promote the national interest rather than toe the party line. With strong civil society support, this forum ensured that some concessions were made, even if there remained important gaps with regards to the level of oversight by civil and political society.

Meanwhile, the dominant ruling coalition in Uganda was proving itself willing to negotiate long and hard with IOCs to secure good deals. The 2014 Memorandum of Understanding between the GoU and its three main investors took over a year to negotiate. In the end, the government won the key battles, particularly around its insistence that the first oil to flow would go first to a refinery rather than out of the country for export via a pipeline, as favoured by the IOCs (Hickey and Izama 2016). The refinery project, designed to ensure that Uganda could add value to its oil locally, reflected a sense in which oil had reinvigorated the president's vision of a self-reliant, nationalist development project for Uganda (Watts 2004). Oil-company representatives involved in the process recounted to us their surprise that the president would personally spend long hours at the negotiating table in pursuit of a good deal for the country, and that he was also willing to allow his oil technocrats the autonomy to perform their role. The results were clear in terms of the upstream fiscal regime that each country managed to establish. Ghana was able to secure fairly good deals and secure a profit share for government of 38–50 per cent—that is, above the average achieved on the continent; but Uganda gained a higher take of 43.5–66 per cent, which matches international averages (Amoako-Tuffuor and Owusu-Ayim 2010). Even where the same oil company was involved in both countries, the GoU secured a much higher proportion of post-cost-recovery proceeds than the government of Ghana and also established limitations on the level of cost recovery available to IOCs, which Ghana failed to do (Hickey et al. 2020). Independent civil society organizations normally highly critical of Uganda's approach to governing oil accepted that the deals it managed to secure would yield impressively high returns should production reach peak levels (Global Witness 2014).

The Role of Pockets of Effectiveness (PoEs) in Governing Oil

An important explanation for this divergence lies in the relative autonomy and capacity that charactterised oil technocrats in each different type of political settlement. In Uganda, a patriotic and highly trained set of oil technocrats, in charge of the Petroleum Exploration and Production Department (PEPD) within the Ministry of Energy and Mineral Development, were key players in this story. The president had established this unit back in 1986, when it became clear that the country lacked the relevant cadre of trained scientists required to identify, develop, and manage the country's natural resources. Unwilling to hand over control to the IOCs, despite their offers to develop the sector, the president sent Ugandans abroad for training and shielded them from the political pressures of patronage that beset most other aspects of the public sector in Uganda. PEPD was led by highly patriotic and committed geoscientists through the long and often fruitless years of exploration. Eventually, these efforts plus financial support from the World Bank and then also Norway and India enabled PEPD to recruit and train staff and acquire enough data to attract big industry players (Kashambuzi 2010: 3).

PEPD came to be characterized by high levels of human-resource capacity, with all operational and senior staff holding postgraduate degrees in relevant fields while also receiving regular on-the-job training. It's largely meritocratic processes of recruitment and promotion were protected from external political influence, and staff are incentivized through their high salaries, allowances, technical support, and considerable autonomy. Importantly, Uganda's dominant political settlement afforded PEPD a high degree of continuity and political protection. After 2006, when commercial quantities of oil were discovered, a strikingly close relationship developed between the president and senior technocrats within the PEPD, which became something of a presidential think tank on oil. This was contrasted with the president's general approach to the public bureaucracy over this period, which was largely to sidestep it in favour of establishing parallel structures and more personalized forms of governance (Kjær 2015; Golooba-Mutebi and Hickey 2016), an anomaly to which we return below.

In contrast, the equivalent organization in Ghana seemed by the mid-2010s to have become mired in the politics of competitive clientelism. The origins of the Ghana National Petroleum Corporation (GNPC) are similar to that of PEPD, in that it was established in 1984 during a period of dominant rule and under a leadership with resource nationalist intentions—namely, the Provisional National Defence Council (PNDC) government of President Rawlings. Significant efforts were initially made to develop the capacity of the GNPC to undertake exploration and attract foreign investment, with officials sent abroad to acquire higher degrees in petroleum-related subjects, including to Canada, the United Kingdom, Romania, and Russia (interview, GNPC official, 27 August 2014), and attached to IOCs in order to build capacity around project management and contract negotiations. Staff spoke of being highly motivated by the professional development opportunities and relatively high salaries available at GNPC, as well as alignment with PNDC's ideological commitment to development at the time. It too gained international admiration for the capacity of its technocrats during its early phase of operations and was even hired to undertake activities within the oil sectors of other African countries.

However, its close links to the PNDC (later NDC) meant that it was viewed with suspicion by the opposition NPP party when it arrived into power in 2000 (Hickey et al. 2020). The new government undertook a significant restructuring of the corporation, which saw its leader imprisoned and 90 per cent of GNPC staff sacked. The move was generally perceived as politically motivated, with one ministry official referring to a 'political agenda rather than a developmental agenda' at work. This meant that the early deals with oil companies in Ghana were established by the president and his advisors rather than by the country's leading oil technocrats. Some of these have had to be overruled, in part through concerns that deals were offered to firms with ruling party links. The fortunes of the GNPC were reversed somewhat after 2008, with the NDC returning to power and investing heavily in recruitment and capacity-building projects within the GNPC, which by 2016 had started to generate increasingly significant revenue flows for reinvestment in the oil industry and the broader economy (Asante et al. 2021). However, further evidence of the boom and bust to which public-sector agencies can be subjected within competitive clientelist settlements emerged after the 2016 elections, with the returning NPP government once again seeking to reduce GNPC's capacity and role in the sector (Asante et al. 2021).

Importantly, our analysis does not lead us to predict that Uganda's better deals will necessarily mean that it will reap higher society-wide dividends from oil than will Ghana. Much else will define this, including shifting oil prices and how far governments are able to restrain oil companies with regards to cost recovery, as well as political settlement dynamics over time. The increasingly personalized and contested nature of political dominance in Uganda raises concerns regarding the extent to which the scenario we describe here will persist over the medium term, and whether the close relationship between president and bureaucrats may tip over into collusion. Given how poorly GoU is performing in relation to other developmental challenges, it may be that the forms of oil governance considered here constitute a special case, partly because upstream tasks such as deal-making are more amenable to being controlled by narrow coalitions of politicians and bureaucrats, and partly because hydrocarbon development requires long-term investments and planning of the type suited to dominant ruling coalitions that hold power over prolonged periods.

Implications for Theory and Practice

The findings presented here offer strong support for our claims that a power domains analysis can offer more relevant and accurate insights into the politics of natural-resource governance than a more limited institutionalist perspective. Indeed, there is growing evidence that political settlements analysis can provide more compelling explanations than new institutionalism with regards to how countries actually govern their new oil and gas finds (Karl 2007; Lewis 2007; Poteete 2009; Hickey and Izama 2016; Bebbington et al. 2018; Macuane et al. 2018; Mohan et al. 2018), and can help to underpin a more relevant and 'politically attuned' policy agenda for natural resource governance.

The critical role that such bureaucratic 'pockets of effectiveness' (PoEs) can play in offering developmental forms of governance in even the most unpromising governance contexts has become increasingly recognized within discussions of oil governance, and more broadly (Roll 2014; and see Chapter 6). Acting as agile repositories of state capacity and elite commitment, 'embedded autonomy' is a critical characteristic of these PoEs (Evans 1995), which receive political protection and capacity-building support while also being afforded the autonomy to conduct their roles in a largely technocratic manner (Fukuyama 2013). The growing literature on PoEs, particularly in the field of oil governance (e.g. Lewis 2007; Hertog 2010; Hout 2013), converges with our finding here that they are more likely to be protected and sustained in dominant settings, where implementation capacities, long-term vision, and stability may be at higher levels, and that increased levels of competition within both competitive clientelist settings and weak dominant settings make it very difficult to protect and sustain such PoEs. This may be particularly the case with policy challenges that are located at the upper end of the value chain within the domain of oil governance, and that can be handled by relatively small numbers of expert bureaucrats. We subject this proposition to further scrutiny in Chapter 6, where we examine the role of PoEs within the economic policy realm of five African countries.

This suggests that efforts to promote system-wide processes of bureaucratic reform may be unnecessary as well as unrealistic in many developing country contexts (Levy 2014). The role of PoEs also seems to be in line with current calls for a new governance agenda, one focused on solving particular problems in particular contexts (Andrews 2013), and we would agree that international support can play an important role here, as through well-targeted capacity-building from highly experienced oil-producing nations, and the incorporation of technocrats into epistemic communities that can help build both technical excellence and professional norms. However, domestic forms of power and politics remain critical, suggesting not merely that reforms need to 'fit' particular contexts, but that external interventions need to be closely attuned to the dominant ideas and incentives generated within particular *types* of political settlement, and in particular to the interplay of political power and state capacity therein (Thurber et al. 2011).

4

Rights and Recognition Puzzles

When Do Elites Commit to Protecting Vulnerable Citizens?

Inclusive development extends beyond processes of economic development to wider aspects of human flourishing, including the need for people to be protected from the various vulnerabilities that all humans are subject to. In this chapter we try to identify the conditions under which ruling elites agree to invest in protecting vulnerable and excluded groups by distributing non-contributory forms of social assistance and by passing legislation to protect women from domestic violence (DV).

Social Assistance: When Do Elites Support Policy against Poverty and Vulnerability?

The spread of social assistance interventions in the global south has been termed a 'quiet revolution' (Hanlon et al. 2010: 4).[1] By 2016, over 130 middle- and low-income countries had at least one non-contributory cash transfer project, including twice as many countries in Africa as was the case in 2010 (ODI 2016). Much of this is the result of concerted efforts since the early 2000s by transnational development actors to position social protection as a new global public-policy agenda (Hickey and Seekings 2019). This move was driven in part by successive crises within the global economy: first, the financial crisis of the late 1990s in Southeast and East Asia helped break the Washington Consensus and heralded an ideological shift among international development agencies towards the Post-Washington Consensus around a more 'inclusive neoliberalism' (Craig and Porter 2006); the next

[1] This section draws on work coordinated jointly for ESID by Sam Hickey and Tom Lavers, some of which is reported in Hickey et al. (2019). Their more recent work on the politics of social protection has been updated with new evidence, extended to include a larger sample of eight countries and also a stronger focus on how cash transfer programmes have become institutionalized over time (see Lavers and Hickey 2022). These differences have also meant that the evidence and analysis presented here differ somewhat from those presented in Lavers and Hickey (2022)—e.g. further developments have seen Kenya and Zambia extend their provision to levels more comparable with Ethiopia and Rwanda. On the politics of implementing rather than adopting social protection, see Lavers (2022).

Pathways to Development. Sam Hickey and Kunal Sen, Oxford University Press.
 DOI: 10.1093/oso/9780198872566.003.0004

and more global financial crisis of 2007–8 would see a major spike in actual expenditures on social protection programmes in the global south. Although social protection had long been a policy agenda for some international actors, most notably the International Labour Organization (ILO) with its historic focus on social insurance and labour-market interventions (Norton et al. 2001; Deacon 2003), it was only in the 2000s that social protection attained the status of a global policy agenda.

The World Bank moved strongly into this field in the early 2000s, inspired by the success of conditional cash transfers in Brazil and Mexico in particular (Peck and Theodore 2015). The UK's Department for International Development (DFID) followed shortly afterwards, influenced not only by the Latin American experience but also by the sense of its advisors in drought-stricken parts of Africa that new and more permanent forms of response to recurrent humanitarian crises were required (Hickey and Seekings 2019). The list of interested parties continued to grow, and, by the end of the 2000s, the United Nations Children's Fund (UNICEF), Food and Agriculture Organization (FAO), and World Food Programme (WFP) were all funding cash transfer programmes in developing countries. By 2012 even the International Monetary Fund (IMF) acknowledged that social protection was required if development was to be inclusive, and by 2015 social protection was firmly inscribed within several Sustainable Development Goals. This new policy agenda was actively promoted not only by a wide range of international agencies but also by a growing 'epistemic community' of policy entrepreneurs, researchers, think tanks, and civil society organizations. Driven by aid agency finance and key officials and advisors working within the World Bank, DFID, and sometimes also UNICEF, these actors moved swiftly to encourage governments in Africa to adopt pilot cash transfer programmes. Although aid conditionality was sometimes used here, the dominant methods were those of persuasion, including efforts to build policy coalitions with bureaucrats from the relevant government departments, the generation of evidence on the potential for cash transfer programmes to be successful in Africa, the organization of international events to discuss and promote social assistance, and also of study tours to enable senior government officials to witness the potential of cash transfers first hand (Hickey and Seekings 2019).

This significant international effort to promote social assistance in developing countries has led some observers to suggest that the spread of social assistance programmes in Africa has been primarily driven by external factors (e.g. von Gliszczynski 2015; Simpson 2017). However, a closer examination of the patterns of expenditure on social protection in Africa, and the level of institutional commitment to it within particular countries, reveals that the spread of social protection is highly uneven, with some countries going much further than others in embedding and rolling out social protection than others. The large literature on how welfare regimes develop suggests a variety of mechanisms through which this takes place, including economic and institutional development, some of which has recently been applied to Africa (Kpessa and Béland 2013). However, our initial efforts to map these uneven expenditures on social protection against standard indicators of economic growth, structural transformation, state capacity, and levels of democracy revealed no clear patterns. More democratic countries, those with higher levels of economic growth or structural transformation, and those with greater state capacity seem no more likely than their less successful counterparts to invest in protecting their citizens.[2] Unlike in Latin America, it did not seem that democratization was necessarily helping to drive up political support for social protection in Africa (Brooks 2015).

To try and understand what was happening here, we investigated the processes through which five countries in Africa adopted social assistance interventions from the mid-2000s onwards.[3] Our evidence and analysis revealed that the global roll-out of social assistance has been a highly contested process, heavily mediated by domestic political dynamics and struggles over ideas. The types of political settlement in place in different countries, and the shifting dynamics of power relations involving elites and citizens, have directly shaped the levels of commitment to social assistance that have emerged, and the extent to which transnational efforts to build advocacy coalitions within this new policy domain have been effective.

Table 4.1 shows the differing levels of elite commitment to social assistance in our cases, using indicators that go beyond expenditure to include other important aspects, such as the capacity and credibility of the part of government where social assistance has been located, how far social assistance has been integrated within a country's overall development strategy, and the degree of effort put into securing implementation. The top performers, not only in terms of levels of commitment but also in terms of being early adopters and the pace at which interventions have been rolled out, are Ethiopia and Rwanda. Kenya occupies the middle ground, in that it has relatively low levels of expenditure, but has gone further than most in terms of

[2] This involved correlating government expenditure on social protection from ILO (2014) data with data on GDP growth (World Bank), democracy (Polity IV), and governance (WGI) and structural transformation (Hidalgo and Hausmann's measure (2009) of economic complexity). The simple regressions we ran individually on each of these independent variables failed to produce an R^2 of more than 0.16.

[3] This research deployed a version of the power domains framework especially adapted for social protection (Lavers and Hickey 2016).

institutionalizing its commitment to social assistance through constitutional and legislative measures. Further down we find Zambia and Uganda, both countries where social assistance initiatives have been established, but in ways that were (at the time of our research) somewhat piecemeal and poorly integrated within each country's respective development strategy, and where external pressure from donors played a highly significant role.

What has driven this unevenness? The role of international development actors can explain only part of the story here, given that pretty much the same set of international players (particularly DFID, UNICEF, and the World Bank) were actively involved in all five of our countries over the same time period. As Table 4.2 on the drivers of elite commitment to social assistance reveals, international efforts to build policy coalitions in favour of social assistance were neither a necessary nor a sufficient condition for social assistance programmes to move beyond pilot projects into wider roll-outs. Although these efforts were critical in securing a place for social assistance on the policy agenda, whether or not they featured on the political agenda, and at what level of importance, was clearly driven by the nature and dynamics of the political settlement in each case. Interestingly, one of the donor agencies most centrally involved in promoting social assistance within Africa, the UK's DFID, realized that this was the challenge and sought to adopt many of the principles of 'thinking and working politically' in its bid to promote social assistance. This involved going beyond the usual provision of technical and financial assistance for policy development and project design: DFID commissioned political economy studies of the social assistance domain and used these to identify key sources of resistance and support, to build coalitions of supporters for social assistance among bureaucrats, politicians, and civil society actors, and to reframe the language of social assistance in ways that resonated with elite ideas around deservingness and sought to offset their concerns with dependency (Hickey and Bukenya 2019b; Pruce and Hickey 2019). As discussed below, this helped to ensure that policy ideas around cash transfers became aligned with paradigmatic ideas in ways that eventually persuaded some elites to support them.

The Domestic Political Economy of Social Cash Transfers

A simple glance at the *types* of countries with the highest levels of commitment to social assistance, and the capacity to implement it effectively with relatively little interference from patronage politics, suggests that dominant political settlements are outperforming their more competitive counterparts.

Ethiopia and Rwanda both moved earlier than their counterparts to adopt social assistance, swiftly translating this new policy agenda into a model that made sense within the context of their own productivist development strategy, rather than simply adopting externally promoted models. Ethiopia led the way here in 2004 as it sought to identify a more permanent response to periodic crises of drought-induced food insecurity. Although lobbied strongly by international actors to adopt cash transfers, it instead introduced a large public works programme that included a relatively small cash transfer component for the less able-bodied and that would be run by government agencies (Lavers 2019a). Rwanda borrowed directly from this experience, establishing a similar programme that was also rolled out rapidly (Lavers 2019b). International actors helped to design and finance the schemes, but national politicians and bureaucrats were clearly in charge of the process in both countries. The longer-term horizons of elites in dominant settings, and the capacity to push through and implement reforms effectively, both seem to have played significant roles here, as did the sense that social assistance was considered important to maintaining legitimacy for dominant coalitions involved in trading-off development progress against political freedoms.

However, the political settlements story around cash transfers cannot be reduced to the issue of dominance. Rather, the strongest predictor of the level of elite commitment to social assistance comes from the nature of political settlement *dynamics*, including with regards the social configuration of particular settlements. What mattered most was the extent to which ruling elites perceived shifting patterns of power relations to constitute a threat to the political settlement, and their role within it, during the period over which cash transfers were being promoted as a new global public policy. The greater the threat was perceived to be, the stronger the response. For example, successive crises of food insecurity in Ethiopia came to be seen as a threat to national security that had to be dealt with as a matter of urgency (Lavers 2019a). This coincided with an important shift within the ruling coalition, whereby the faction within the broad coalition led by the prime minister became more dominant, in part through the departure of a more radical faction whose developmental ideas prohibited a focus on welfare 'handouts'. In Rwanda, senior politicians and bureaucrats were galvanized into searching for a solution when annual statistics in 2007 showed that the rate of poverty reduction had slowed, particularly in regions predominantly populated by the majority Hutu. For a ruling coalition dominated by members of a minority ethnic group that had pinned its legitimacy on being seen to provide inclusive development in a post-genocide setting, this constituted a threat to its legitimacy that had to be dealt with (Lavers 2019b).

In our other, more competitive countries, governments were generally slower to adopt social assistance programmes at scale. Although lobbied hard by international actors from the early 2000s, ruling elites largely restricted the spread of cash transfers to small pilot programmes for nearly a decade. This was in part because they were not persuaded that they were facing a crisis within their political settlements to which cash transfers constituted a rational response. When political settlement dynamics did finally shift in Uganda and Zambia, in ways that persuaded elites of the logics of cash transfers, these shifts did not involve existential threats to the political settlement, as in the case of Ethiopia and Rwanda, but were instead catalysed by political settlement dynamics operating at a lower level. In Zambia, the president was persuaded to massively increase expenditures on social assistance by a crisis with one of the mechanisms of clientelism through which elites distributed goods to rural areas. In 2013, the main agricultural subsidy and food security programmes that ruling elites had traditionally used to secure support in rural areas (Mason et al. 2013) were hugely overspent (Pruce and Hickey 2019). Searching for an alternative means to maintain legitimacy in rural areas, and to deliver on 2011 manifesto promises to reduce poverty, the then president was persuaded by certain bureaucrats that cash transfers would offer a more effective method of reaching poor households than the subsidies programmes. These bureaucrats formed part of a pro-social protection policy coalition that had been established by donors nearly a decade earlier in the mid-2000s. Informed by political economy analysis of the social protection domain in Zambia, this coalition had begun to build a systematic body of evidence, including through the use of randomized control trials, to support the case for cash transfers (Quarles van Ufford et al. 2016). At the same time, and in true 'thinking-and-working politically' style (Booth 2015), the coalition worked through an arm's-length broker capable of accessing senior government officials and convening then to consider these findings at a Cabinet retreat in 2013, immediately prior to the announcement. Confronted with both a mini-distributional crisis and a credible policy case, the president ordered a 700 per cent increase in the budget for cash transfers (Pruce and Hickey 2019).

In Uganda, a similar transnational policy coalition also eventually managed to achieve an alignment between its promotion of social assistance and domestic political settlement dynamics, largely through establishing a pilot social pension project in 14 of Uganda's 112 districts in 2010. By 2012, this project had helped catalyse demand-making activities from people not included in the project, particularly from those in districts that neighboured districts that were benefiting from the transfer (Hickey and Bukenya 2019a).

Importantly, one such district lay in the historically oppositional northern part of the country, where the president was keen to consolidate his electoral support. This occurred within a broader context in which elite defections and the longer-term effects of persistent clientelism had deepened a tendency towards populist and personalized policy responses (see Appendix II, country summaries). On receiving the demands from elders at his country residence, he wrote a letter to the Minister of Gender in 2013, ordering her to include this new district in the pilot project and to prepare plans for a national roll-out. In Zambia and particularly in Uganda, these lower-order political settlement dynamics—which catalysed a sense of existential crisis among elites regarding the status not of the settlement itself but rather of the distributive mechanisms through which they maintained themselves in power—generated lower levels of commitment. This is evidenced by the ways in which policy responses were poorly integrated within mainstream development strategies and delivered by weak rather than core parts of the state apparatus: while ministries of social welfare took the lead in Uganda and Zambia, the more powerful ministries of agriculture and local government were deployed in Ethiopia and Rwanda respectively.

The case of Kenya is the only one of our cases where competitive elections helped persuade ruling elites of the logic of cash transfers, with an apparently more minor role for the existential threat created by a crisis within regular political settlement dynamics. In the build-up to the 2002 elections, UNICEF persuaded key members of the then opposition party to adopt cash transfers as part of their platform (Wanyama and McCord 2017). Once the National Rainbow coalition took power, UNICEF lobbied them to make good on this commitment to implement a child grant for orphans and vulnerable children. This provision was then scaled up again at the 2007 election, which was also highly competitive and won by the same president. It seems plausible that the post-election violence that followed may have further catalysed a perception among elites that they needed to reach out to voters, with the constitutional reforms that followed including a commitment to social assistance, although few of our respondents suggested this directly. The further expansion of social assistance programmes after both the 2013 and 2017 elections further emphasizes the extent to which competitive politics can, in some cases in Africa at least, be a driver of the rapid expansion of the three main social transfer programmes. Although both Uganda and Zambia are now characterized by competitive elections, the initial decisions to scale up social assistance coverage in these cases occurred during the middle of electoral cycles and can be more directly traced to the other political settlement dynamics, as suggested above. However, the fact that Africa contains many

Table 4.1 Indicators of elite commitment to social assistance

Case	Time period	Financial commitments	Involvement of key politicians and ministry	Legal basis for policy	Government implementation	Integrated into development strategy	Coverage	Elite commitment*
Ethiopia PSNP	2001–2	0	0	0	0	0	0	0 (None)
	2003–19	0.5	1	0	1	1	1	4.5 (Strong)
Ethiopia UPSNP	2001–5	0	0	0	0	0	0	0 (None)
	2014–19	1	0.5	0	1	1	0.5	4 (Strong)
Rwanda VUP	2000–6	0	0	0	0	0	0	0 (None)
	2007–19	1	1	0	1	1	0.5	4.5 (Strong)
Kenya	Pre-2003	0	0	0	0	0	0	0 (None)
	2003–7	0	0	0	1	0	0	1 (Weak)
	2008–19	1	0	0.5	1	0	0.5	3 (Moderate)
Uganda	Pre-2007	0	0	0	0	0	0	0 (None)
	2007–11	0	0	0	0.5	0	0	0.5 (Weak)
	2014–19	0.5	0.5	0	0.5	0	0	1.5 (Weak)
Zambia	Pre-2003	0	0	0	0	0	0	0 (None)
	2003–13	0	0	0	0.5	0	0	0.5 (Weak)
	2013–19	0.5	0	0	1	0	0.5	2 (Moderate)

* None: 0; Weak: 0.5–1.5; Moderate 2–3.5; Strong 4–6.
Note: The year of research is 2019.
Source: authors.

Table 4.2 Drivers of social assistance in Africa

Cases	Dominant political settlement?	PS dynamics: significant shift or threat?	Donors: coherent policy coalition?	Outcome
Rwanda	Y	Y	N	Strong commitment, delivered impartially
Ethiopia	Y	Y	Y	Strong commitment, delivered impartially
Kenya	N	Y	Y	Commitment, delivered as patronage
Zambia	N	N	Y	Limited commitment, delivered as patronage
Uganda	Y	N	Y	Limited commitment, delivered as patronage

Source: authors.

countries with competitive elections suggests this route may increasingly become an important driver of the social assistance expansion.

Finally, political settlement types have also shaped the ways in which social assistance has been delivered in Africa. Multiple evaluations have found the programmes in Ethiopia and Rwanda to be delivered relatively effectively and without bias with regards to questions of ethnic or political loyalty (e.g. Devereux and Ulrichs 2015). This stands in contrast to the overtly political use of cash transfers in Uganda, where the post-pilot roll-out phase, which targeted the 100 poorest residents in 40 districts by 2020, is informed by the distributional logic of patronage politics rather than technically informed or pro-poor targeting. Kenya seems to represent an interesting compromise here. While the majority of the transfers allocated are distributed according to need, the remaining 30 per cent go to all of Kenya's constituencies, apparently to ensure that all parliamentarians are able to associate themselves with this act of state largesse. This range of responses suggests that whether social assistance is heralding the onset of a new social contract or re-embedding the logics of clientelism within Africa remains an open question and one that will be defined by the interactions of political settlement dynamics and this new, highly transnationalized policy domain.

Anti-domestic-violence Legislation: When Do Elites Support Policy Protecting Vulnerable Groups?

Women's political empowerment remains a highly contested process across the world, with female inclusion in formal politics rising significantly in some regions, while facing blockages and backsliding elsewhere.[4] Importantly, progress towards greater political inclusion has not always yielded progress in terms of the passage of legislation aimed at promoting women's rights and gender equity—particularly where this involves a challenge to existing gender relations and male privilege, including on reproductive rights, domestic violence (DV), and land rights (Basu 2010; Waylen 2012). Thus, any assumptions that 'inclusion' would necessarily lead to 'influence' turned out to be complacent (Goetz and Hassim 2003). Moreover, the tendency to assume women's political inclusion as the primary driver of gender-equity policy (Escobar-Lemmon and Taylor-Robinson 2014) works to instrumentalize women's participation—recasting it as only a means to an end rather than as an important goal of gender equity in itself—while also overlooking some of the broader political drivers of progress.

This project attempted to move beyond these limitations. Here, we do examine the politics of women's political inclusion, and its links to legislation against DV, but also explore the wider relationship between the political settlement and the 'policy domain' of women's interests and rights. Our evidence on both the progress of women's political inclusion and gender-equity policies shows that both have primarily been shaped by the interaction between different types of political settlement—and shifting political settlement dynamics—on the one hand, and the role of coalitions within the domain of women's interests, on the other (Nazneen et al. 2019).

The Cases

The project used a process-tracing methodology in six cases followed by comparative analysis, aiming to find a useful midpoint between catch-all generalization and 'context-is-everything' specificity, and to uncover causal pathways rather than merely correlations. The cases fall broadly into two groups: the dominant-type political settlements of Rwanda, Uganda, and South Africa, and the more competitive settlements of Bangladesh, Ghana, and India. All six introduced DV legislation in the period from 1998 (South Africa) to 2010 (Bangladesh and Uganda), with India (2005), Ghana (2007), and Rwanda (2008) in between. Our interest was in the process both leading up to and immediately following the moment of lawmaking.

[4] This section draws on a comparative project coordinated by Sohela Nazneen, involving country-level studies led by herself (Bangladesh), Beatrix Allah-Mensah and Rhoda Osei-Afful (Ghana), Asmita Basu (India), Jennie Burnet (Rwanda), Lillian Artz (South Africa), and Josephine Ahikire and Amon Mwiine (Uganda), plus global-level analysis by Sophie King and Eleni Sifaki. The fuller results are presented in Nazneen, Hickey, and Sifaki (2019).

There are important similarities between the three dominant-type countries as compared to the three competitive-type countries. The dominant coalitions in Rwanda, Uganda, and South Africa each took two or three years to pass legislation in response to activism, whereas it was four, five, and twelve years in the competitive–clientelist settings of Bangladesh, Ghana, and India respectively. The former countries introduced implementation plans within one or two years of the law, whereas only one of the latter did (India); it was over three years in Bangladesh and had not yet happened twelve years later in Ghana. In both types, the interaction of political settlements with the domain of women's interests was critical, but in different ways.

In the dominant, somewhat personalized, settlements of Rwanda and Uganda, the support of the president was crucial to the progress of the legislation. In the case of Rwanda, the process to pass the 2008 law was hardly contentious at all. Led by the large cohort of female MPs, and in line with earlier legislative moves to empower women (for instance, regarding co-ownership of land), the process took only two years, because the formal process of consultation with local communities was taken seriously by female MPs (Burnet and d'Arc Kanakuze 2018). The weaker dominance of President Museveni in neighbouring Uganda, and his instrumental rather than ideological commitment to women's rights (Goetz and Hassim 2003), helped ensure that the path to the 2010 law there was much more contested (Ahikire and Mwiine 2019). The Ugandan women's movement played a critical role in eventually gaining presidential support, first through forming a strong civil society coalition, including a strategic alliance with the Catholic Church, and then through extending this with alliances in parliament and the bureaucracy. This was done while seeking to offset strong ideological opposition among a patriarchal ruling elite whose opposition had recently been galvanized by its refusal to pass even more transformative legislation on marital relations and women's co-ownership of land. In the dominant, but more institutionalized, setting of South Africa, the ruling support of the ruling African National Congress (ANC) was similarly important. The Women's National Coalition enjoyed strong links with the ANC, stemming from the anti-apartheid struggle. However, when relations between the two began to fray post-1994, informal alliances between members of the DV policy coalition and the ruling party helped to ease the progress of the proposed DV legislation through South Africa's relatively well-established formal institutional channels to become law in 1998.

By contrast, in the competitive–clientelist countries, activists faced a wider range of both potential allies and opponents, making it harder to know where to focus advocacy efforts. Given the less secure position of ruling elites, some groups opposed to gender-equity measures have considerable sway. In each of Bangladesh, Ghana, and India, powerful conservative religious groups were a major factor affecting how activists framed proposals, spurring a complicated mix of occasional confrontation while trying to avoid provoking determined opposition by reframing demands and seeking co-optation. Moreover, encouraging a programmatic focus on women's rights proved difficult in contexts where political parties were as often vehicles for other identity-based concerns (such as ethno-regional or religious ones) or for personal projects of leaders.

In both Ghana and Bangladesh, women's movements had long struggled to gain traction for their agendas among two main political parties locked in mortal combat for power. A large part of this was because those parties saw little to gain from advancing women's rights, either electorally or in terms of opportunities for the distribution of patronage—the key currency of political exchange in both cases.

In Bangladesh, progress was made only once the normal functioning of competitive clientelism was suspended in 2008 to allow a neutral caretaker government to run the general election. This opened a window of opportunity for the women's movement to forge an alliance with state bureaucrats ('femocrats') to advance the policy agenda (Nazneen 2019). Later, when Bangladesh re-entered electoral politics, the process of signing the legislation into law was enabled by the shifting configuration of power around the ruling coalition. On the one hand, the ruling coalition needed to garner support from secular groups (including women's rights groups), while, on the other, the holding power of the religious right was temporarily weakened owing to an ongoing court case that took them out of parliamentary action (Nazneen 2019). There was also a transnational dimension to the decision of the prime minister to advance the legislation in 2010: insiders noted that she did not want to be embarrassed when presenting Bangladesh's progress on the United Nations 'Convention on the Elimination of all Forms of Discrimination against Women' in New York later that same year.

In Ghana, progress was initially blocked by a female Minister for Women's Affairs, before being enabled by her replacement. The women's movement was again important, although its capacity for mobilization had long been weakened by partisan splits and a reliance on the patronage of leading females for making advances (Allah-Mensah and Osei-Afful 2019). Here, progress relied on the issue of DV being politicised during the build-up to the 2008 elections, partly through high-profile cases publicized by the women's movement, which encouraged the opposition party to make political capital out of the sitting government's lack of progress on the issue. The law was passed in 2007.

In India, the DV Act was passed in 2005 following a two-decades-long struggle. The fate of the law was closely tied to which party was in power, and the kinds of informal relations the policy coalition had with specific 'femocrats'. The campaign for DV legislation also coincided with the rise of very conservative 'Hindu nationalists', who became crucial to the ruling coalition. With politicians operating under competitive electoral conditions wary of antagonizing the *Hindutva*, the DV legislation process became extremely protracted. In the 1990s, the women's movement formed a more broad-based coalition, before 2004 finally brought a turning point when a coalition comprising the United Progressive Alliance and some smaller left-leaning parties took over, the latter insisting on the Act as a condition of joining the coalition.

Comparative Analysis

These cases, then, demonstrate how the process of adopting anti-DV legislation in the 1990s and 2000s was strongly shaped by political settlement type and dynamics.

One mechanism was through representation and formal inclusion. The case of Ghana is particularly instructive: although rightly celebrated as a rare example of a consolidated democracy in Africa, its progress on anti-DV measures has been particularly weak, and it also has the second lowest percentage (14 per cent) of female members of parliament of the six countries and has no representation quota (India, the only other country without a quota, is lower, at 8 per cent). This reflects key moments of political settlement formation in Ghana; women's claims for inclusion were not strongly politicized when the current settlement was being formed in the early 1990s, and as a result a quota that had briefly been in place following independence was not reinstated. While women participated in large numbers in India's independence movement, women's issues were somewhat marginal within that movement, continuing a legacy of reformism generally carried out by men (Basu 2019: 172–3). By contrast, in Rwanda, Uganda, Bangladesh, and South Africa, women were able to make strong claims for political inclusion during critical junctures where political settlements were formed, based either on suffering endured during armed conflict (Rwanda during the 1994 genocide; Bangladesh during the war with Pakistan in 1971) and/or on their active role during the struggles that preceded the forging of new settlements (the revolutionary force in early 1990s Rwanda; the guerrilla struggle in early

1980s Uganda; the anti-authoritarian movement in early 1990s Bangladesh; the anti-apartheid movement in pre-1994 South Africa). Thus, one form of influence of the political settlement is through its formative effect on women's representation.

The inclusion of women in politics (especially via quotas; see Table 4.3) may be an explanatory factor in the differing trajectories of DV legislation processes, with progress swifter in countries with higher proportions of female MPs. However, our process-tracing research shows that female MPs were rarely a key element in the fortunes of proposed DV legislation. Instead, the women's movement and key allies in the higher echelons of government were often more significant. Indeed, while women's movements were critical players, what mattered most was their capacity to mobilize coalitions of actors that cut across civil and political society, particularly in terms of forming alliances with powerful actors within parliament and the state bureaucracy, and also across divides within civil society, as between urban and rural women's groups. This required a significant and often highly informal effort: in Uganda, women's activists encouraged female MPs to target powerful male MPs who had an influence in parliament, sitting next to them during sessions where the legislation was being debated and discouraging them from opposing. In Bangladesh, the personal networks between ruling elites, based on ties of family and friendship, were important in securing support (Nazneen 2017). Although generally lacking the social and financial capital to navigate patronage politics, women activists found ways to mobilize informal networks and relationships to their advantage.

Another crucial factor concerns the role of ideas. One aspect of this is that we can draw a causal link to the taking of power by movements possessing an ideological basis in transforming citizenship. In South Africa, following the anti-apartheid struggle and women's role in it, gender equality was central to the ANC's legitimizing narrative. In Rwanda, women's physical security—following devastating recent conflict—was a core legitimizing idea of the RPF. By contrast, the Ugandan NRM's seeming initial commitment to empowering women rapidly turned out to be highly instrumentalized, with female politicians soon becoming treated essentially as a vote bank (Goetz and Hassim 2003).

A second ideational aspect concerned the creative use that feminist activists made of ideas in the discursive strategies that underpinned their campaigns for new legislation. With the partial exception of Rwanda, where the president was already strongly associated with an ideological commitment to promoting women's rights, women's movements had to adapt their discourse to ensure that there was an alignment with more dominant ideas among elites.

In Uganda, Bangladesh, and (eventually) Ghana, the language of 'women's rights' was dropped to avoid a direct confrontation with paradigmatic ideas about gender relations. Women's activists instead reframed the case for anti-DV legislation in terms of 'family values' and 'development', and, in Rwanda, in line with protective rather than patriarchal forms of masculinity, emphasizing men's role as brothers and fathers rather than husbands.[5] This was critical in gaining support from influential religious actors in Ghana and Uganda, where the Archbishop of Uganda based his 2009 Easter address around the need for this legislation. In South Africa a similar element of compromise arose. This was because of the need to work around the opposition of those traditional leaders participating in the post-apartheid settlement process, although even here the women's movement also won some important battles—for instance, arguing down a proposal to excuse customary law from the application of the constitutional equality clause.

Across the six countries, this strategic approach to 'going with the grain' of dominant ideas helped expedite the passing of legislation, but also entailed compromises on various provisions. In Uganda, for instance, the jettisoning of marital rape from the legislation (something that also happened in Ghana and Bangladesh) greatly restricted the extent to which the new laws challenged engrained gender relations and patriarchal ideas of bodily autonomy. The fact that many of the same male MPs in Uganda who were eventually persuaded to support the DV Bill in 2009 would then decisively shoot down the 2013 Marriage and Divorce Bill is emblematic of the lack of any deeper shift in political norms (Ahikire and Mwiine 2019: 79). By contrast, the fact that Rwanda had already passed laws on co-ownership of land in the wake of the genocide enabled the passage of more robust legislation on DV, including a clause criminalizing marital rape.

The role of ideas also had a transnational dimension here. The emergence since the 1990s of a new global norm denouncing violence against women, and the publicization of high-profile examples, helped create an enabling environment for the adoption of DV legislation (King and Sifaki 2019; Nazneen and Hickey 2019: 192–3). Transnational women's movements and the UN were important, particularly with the Convention on the Elimination of all Forms of Discrimination Against Women (CEDAW), and its translation into local contexts by activists.

However, while such ideas and norms influenced feminist campaigners in most cases, this was generally in a diffuse, subtle way. There were few

[5] This strategic deployment of hegemonic ideas to achieve (potentially) counter-hegemonic outcomes fits more with a Scottian than a Gramscian reading of how wars of position are played out by subordinate groups.

Table 4.3 Cross-case comparison of experiences with domestic-violence legislation

				Key causal factors in the legislation advocacy process					
Country	**Political settlement type**	**Policy coalition formed/DV Act/ Implementation**	**Implementation progress**	**Executive commitment to gender equity**	**Political settlement dynamics**	**Women's movement experience**	**Framing strategy**	**Allies in multiple forums**	**Quotas and % of women in parliament (at time of law)**
Rwanda	(Highly) Dominant, somewhat personalized	2005–6; 2008; 2010	Strong	Strong, ideological, and instrumental	Normal parliamentary process	Extensive, positive	Aligned with progressive ideas of dominant actors	Yes	Yes; 56.3%
Uganda	(Weakly) Dominant, personalized	2008; 2010; 2011	Little progress	Medium, instrumental	Elections relevant	Extensive, negative	Aligned with dominant ideas through compromise	Yes	Yes; 36%
South Africa	Dominant, institutionalized	1995; 1998; 1999	Significant advances	Strong, ideological	Post-transition moment	Extensive, positive	Initially challenged dominant ideas, later compromised	Yes	Yes; 30%

Bangladesh	Competitive–clientelist	2007; 2010; 2013	Some progress	Weak, instrumental	Election hiatus, with key opposition undermined	Extensive, mixed	Compromise with dominant ideas	Limited	Yes; 18%
Ghana	Competitive–clientelist	2002–3; 2007;	Little progress	Weak, instrumental	Elections relevant	Limited experience	Initially challenged dominant ideas, later compromised	Limited	No; 14%
India	Competitive–institutionalized	1993–8; 2005; 2006	Significant advances	Medium, ideological	Elections relevant	Extensive, mixed	Challenge to dominant ideas	Yes	No; 8%

Source: authors.

examples of transnational actors directly influencing campaigns, with feminist movements often consciously downplaying their transnational links to avoid accusations of promoting an overbearing 'Western' agenda at odds with local norms. This often included eschewing talk of 'rights'.

More apparent was the important role played by links to regional women's movements and South–South learning. Experiences from the Malaysian feminist movement were important in India, with the Indian experience then translating into Bangladesh. Debates and strategies from the South African feminist movement and their earlier success in passing legislation against DV influenced movements in Uganda, Rwanda, and Ghana.

Finally, a further conclusion to emerge from this study, as in other policy domains, was the crucial importance of paying attention to the politics of the implementation stage. Each of these governments' efforts to implement anti-DV legislation has been directly shaped by the nature of the political settlement and dominant ideas at play in the context. Only in Rwanda's dominant settlement, where ideological commitment was strong and state capacity high, has serious progress been made. Rwanda had funded and established shelters for women suffering from DV in a third of the country's districts within three years of passing the legislation. Bangladesh, with over twelve times the population of Rwanda, had managed to establish shelters in just five of sixty-four districts. Overall, the translation from political agreement and legislation to implementation varied widely. Most starkly, in Ghana, twelve years after the DV Act, there was still no implementation plan, and none of the necessary state-run DV crisis centres had been created. In Uganda, only NGOs have established shelters. This stems in part from the decreased capacity of the state to deliver on development policy since the ruling coalition became weakened by elite defections and personalized forms of patronage, but also reflects the president's instrumental, rather than ideological, commitment to women's rights. In all six countries, though, there is insufficient financial investment in relevant training and infrastructure. This echoes the finding of ESID research on other policy sectors that the implementation phase has its own politics, with the competing interests of political actors introducing as many complications as in the policy adoption stage. This challenge has become harder still, given the new backlash against women's rights that has emerged in recent years (Goetz 2019).

The focus of this study on women's inclusion and gender equity reveals the value of adopting a power domains approach to interrogating the politics of inclusive development, but also makes the case for both adapting and extending it. In terms of adaptation, our analysis reveals the highly gendered character of political settlements. This is not only in the sense of the relative holding power of groups with marginal status vis-à-vis more powerful players, but also regarding the paradigmatic ideas that bind elites to particular rules, institutional arrangements, and policies, and that shape the boundaries of the possible. In terms of extending the framework, meanwhile, our evidence showed that women in our case-study countries have often been reluctant to use the legislation to protect themselves from DV, for fear of reprisals and of breaking valued relationships (Jackson 2003). This suggests the importance of paying more attention to the localized power domains within which reforms hit the ground, and through which they must be filtered before they can change the lives of individuals. Whether individual women feel able and are willing to use anti-DV legislation will depend more on the configuration of power within households, communities, and local government jurisdictions than within national-level political settlements.

5

Social Provisioning Puzzles

How Can Countries Move from Providing Access to Providing High-Quality Social Services?

There is a growing appreciation that social provisioning in the global south is closely shaped by politics, particularly in terms of the level of public expenditure that governments are willing to commit to sectors such as education and health (e.g. Stasavage 2005; Nelson 2007; Carbone 2009). Some of this literature focuses on the same aspects of politics identified in our power-domains framework, including the critical role played by coalitions in ensuring that difficult reforms are pushed through and implemented (e.g. Grindle 2002; Kosack 2012) and the often significant role played by how state and non-state actors relate to each other (Evans and Heller 2015; Cammett and Maclean 2011). However, most attention has focused on issues of expenditure and levels of access to basic services, rather than on the quality of the service that poor people in particular actually receive. In this chapter, we argue that, just as there is a politics to the expansion of social services in the global south, politics also shapes the capacity and commitment of governments to improve the *quality* of basic service delivery. In particular, we suggest that, whereas simply expanding social provisioning is closely aligned with the elite incentives and social foundations common to most political settlements in developing countries, the opposite is often true when it comes to the politics of improving the quality of provision.

From Schooling to Learning? The Politics of the Learning Crisis

The gap between securing improved levels of access to social services and improving the quality of the service being delivered is perhaps most apparent in the 'learning crisis' that afflicts developing countries (Pritchett 2013;

Pathways to Development. Sam Hickey and Kunal Sen, Oxford University Press.
 DOI: 10.1093/oso/9780198872566.003.0005

World Bank 2017).[1] In 2014, it was estimated that at least 250 million of the 650 million primary-school-aged children were not learning basic reading or mathematics; almost half of those children had attended too little to learn much at all, while the other 130 million who were attending were still not attaining even minimum levels of learning (UNESCO 2014). There is growing recognition that the global learning crisis is shaped by political as well as socio-economic and other factors. Major policy actors now share this concern: the World Bank's 2017 *World Development Report*, for example, focuses explicitly on the quality of education and on how it is shaped by political economy. What is less clear, however, is *how* politics matters. Indeed, education remains a relatively neglected subject within political science, and analysis generally focuses on industrialized societies with long-standing education systems, rather than developing countries.

Our research responds to this theoretical and empirical lacuna, focusing on the political factors that shape the extent to which elite actors become committed to adopting and implementing educational reforms aimed at improving learning outcomes. What are the conditions under which elites support policy to tackle this crisis, and what affects the way such attempts play out in practice?

The push towards securing greater access to education from the early 1990s onwards fitted directly with the incentives of political leaders reliant on large, uneducated rural constituencies, and was bankrolled by donors during the heyday of their debt-inspired hegemony in the domain of social policy. Political elites who had themselves benefited from education also saw it as important for even the poorest citizens, in part because it offers a more governable citizenry and a sense of becoming a more capable modern nation (Hossain 2017). By contrast, the same political dynamics are not yet in place in support of efforts to improve the *quality* of educational provision. This relates in part to the types of policy challenge involved in this aspect of the educational policy domain. Improving levels of access constitutes what can be termed a 'logistical' policy challenge (Andrews et al. 2012)—one that can be delivered through relatively simple political and bureaucratic processes, such as increasing expenditure, employing more teachers, and building more schools—all activities with strong political pay-offs. In contrast, improving the quality of education that children receive is a highly 'transactional' policy challenge (Andrews et al. 2012), requiring the behaviour of frontline bureaucrats and service providers to change in ways that may go against

[1] This section draws on a comparative project coordinated by Sam Hickey, involving country-level studies led by Naomi Hossain (Bangladesh), Tim Kelsall (Cambodia), Franklin Oduro and Edward Ampratwum (Ghana), Tim Williams (Rwanda), Brian Levy (South Africa), and Anne-Mette Kjaer and Suzie Nansozi (Uganda). The fuller results are presented in Hickey and Hossain (2019).

their interests, and ensuring multiple and repeated encounters between these teachers and learners. As discussed below, the political drivers to resolve this type of policy challenge are generally far weaker in developing countries.

We explored the politics of learning in six countries, with case studies of Cambodia and South Africa as well as our usual four of Bangladesh, Ghana, Rwanda, and Uganda. All achieved rapid rates of expansion in the education domain during the 1990s and early 2000s. However, the rate of improvement in terms of learning outcomes has been less even, and slower, particularly in Rwanda and certain regions of South Africa (UNESCO 2014).[2] Repetition rates have risen in Rwanda, Uganda, and Bangladesh since the early 2000s, and, while each case has seen some improvements in terms of certain examination results, these are incommensurate with the significant improvement in educational access. In Cambodia, a 2010 Early Grade Reading Assessment found that one-third of children could not read at all, and, of those who could, almost half had difficulty understanding what they read. There is also a great deal of variation in achievement levels within each country, which again suggests a lack of systematic support for improving quality in this domain. For example, only 38 per cent of Ugandan children passed both numeracy and literacy tests, by some way the lowest in the East Africa region, and average performance varied widely across the country, ranging from 64 per cent in Kampala in Central Region to 15 per cent in Moroto in Northern Region (UWEZO 2012). According to the 2007 round of Southern and Eastern African Consortium for Monitoring Educational Quality, South African students ranked tenth of fourteen countries for reading and eighth for mathematics, behind Tanzania, Kenya, and Swaziland; more than a quarter of Grade 6 students could not read and understand a simple text, ranging from 5 per cent in the Western Cape to 49 per cent in Limpopo.

Our cases demonstrate that political settlements have a significant and direct bearing on educational quality. This is largely because the education domain serves both as a resource base from which rents can be distributed and relationships of patronage maintained and as a means of conferring popular legitimacy on the ruling coalition. Both political functions directly influence the commitment to providing high-quality education (see Table 5.2). The extent to which education comes to form part of a 'rent management system' is greater within political settlements where ruling coalitions are weak relative to lower-level factions. In competitive–clientelist Bangladesh and Ghana, and weakly dominant Uganda, we found strong

[2] Comparative data on educational outcomes are notoriously scarce and left us unable to construct a clear and comparable sense of the progress made over time by our case-study countries. However, see statistical data provided by UNESCO (2014) for some illustration, and on which we base these comments.

evidence of rent-seeking behaviour at multiple levels, including the partisan award of jobs. In such settings, ruling coalitions are also reluctant to promote reforms that involve disciplining politically important and well-organized social actors, such as teachers and their unions. In terms of securing and maintaining legitimacy, the need for governments to appear to be ruling in the interests of all citizens can lead to populist policies—such as universal access to education or enabling free schooling—which, while popular, do not necessarily improve the quality of education. This dynamic occurs in all forms of political settlement, with the president of Rwanda Paul Kagame—often held up as a leader surprisingly immune to the temptations of political expediency—as susceptible as his counterparts to launching fresh drives to improve access at election time (Williams 2017). Indeed, these problems may be deepened in contexts where dominant leaders prevail, as in the case of Uganda, where a long-standing populist promise to keep primary education 'free' has reduced the scope for schools and districts to generate the resources required to offer higher-quality education, or for this policy to be challenged where the originator remains entrenched in power (Kjær and Muwanga 2017). Dominance makes it difficult to challenge questionable policies. In Rwanda, the ambition of the Rwandan Patriotic Front (RPF) for to the country to advance its status as a modern player in the global economy may actually have undermined progress in this regard: one of the main reasons that learning outcomes have been slow to improve was President Kagame's decision to switch the language of instruction from French to English in 2009, despite the fact that only a very small minority of the teaching profession were able to teach proficiently in English at the time.

Dominant political settlements also seem to struggle to deal with the particular type of policy challenge involved in securing improved learning outcomes. Whilst the top-down and hierarchical mechanisms of accountability favoured within many dominant party settlements might be highly effective in delivering on logistical policy challenges, they are poorly suited to addressing more transactional policy challenges that involve multiple stakeholders and information flows (Andrews et al. 2012). In Rwanda, officials within the education sector are used extensively by central government to gather accountability data on local government officials in other policy domains. This process that is critical to the system of upwards accountability in Rwanda, and which as we see below can help drive progressive development outcomes in other domains, but that distracts from their capacity directly improve to performance in their own domain of education (Williams 2017). The example of South Africa's Western Cape (see below) provides further support for this argument, in that, although a relative success story within the country, this province compares poorly with African counterparts in much poorer countries, including Kenya (Levy et al. 2018). This suggests that a functioning hierarchical, impersonal bureaucracy may work very well for certain policy tasks, but that promoting better learning outcomes might be the kind of transactional activity that hierarchical governance arrangements struggle with, and that require mores 'horizontal' and localized mechanisms of accountability and authority (Levy et al. 2018; see also Pritchett 2013).

The fact that competitive pressures alone do not help to predict elite orientations towards this policy challenge further suggests that the configuration of political power within particular settlements may not hold the key to understanding progress when it comes to providing high-quality services in this domain. Faced with similar levels of opposition at the ballot box in the past 2010s (see Appendix II, country summaries), the erstwhile dominant ruling coalitions in Cambodia and Uganda have responded very differently. For example, whereas the Cambodian People's Party (CPP) in Cambodia has appointed technocrats to lead the education ministry in order to placate growing social demands for change, the president in Uganda instead chose to award this brief to his wife (an ambitious politician with little experience within the domain). The key here may rest with the social rather than the political configuration of power in a political settlement. Recent research into the political economy of education has argued that ruling elites will be incentivized to upgrade their educational provision only once a process of structural transformation in the economy has produced demands from capitalists for a more skilled workforce (Doner and Schneider 2016). Given that none of the six countries studied here has moved definitively towards high levels of structural transformation, it is perhaps not surprising that we found political leaders launching successive waves of educational reforms that emphasized delivering visible public goods with which they could be directly associated, rather than the more intangible work involved in ensuring that teachers receive high-quality training and remain on-task in the classroom. However, the country that seems to be taking issues of educational quality most seriously, namely Cambodia, is also the one that has moved furthest towards achieving structural transformation, and where there is some nascent evidence of capitalists placing pressure on political elites to deliver a higher-quality workforce (Kelsall et al. 2019).

Elsewhere in our sample, and even where ruling elites perceive themselves to be under an existential threat that requires the delivery of broad-based services across the country, as in Rwanda, there are few incentives to improve the quality of these services. The largely poor and rural constituency upon which such ruling coalitions rest are not making such demands in a powerful manner. Moreover, the middle-class parents who are more likely to do so have already exited the public sphere of education and generally have a weaker voice within such ruling coalitions.

Educational outcomes also differ according to the local-level context, and this finding suggests that we need to look beyond national political settlements to examine the configuration of power at more local levels, particularly within decentralized systems of educational provision. To explore this phenomenon, we identified high- and low-performing schools in otherwise similar contexts (e.g. urban–rural location, socio-economic status, ethnic composition) and investigated the local political drivers of this divergence. In Ghana, our comparison of two districts in the same region reproduced a political settlements explanation in microcosm. The relative dominance of the ruling party in one district seemed to enable a longer-term perspective among a coalition of local elites with regards to driving up learning outcomes through a difficult reform process, whereas higher levels of electoral competition in the other district had perpetuated a short-termist approach and a reluctance to discipline a teaching workforce critical to maintaining the party's support base.

A comparative analysis of the performance of school systems in the Western and Eastern Cape provinces in South Africa was a particularly illuminating subnational comparison, underscoring the significance of sectoral or domain governance in explaining learning outcomes (Levy et al. 2018). Formally, all nine provinces of South Africa have identical institutional arrangements, stemming from the 1994 Constitution. Similarly, both provincial school systems (in the Western Cape and Eastern Cape) are regulated by the same national policy framework and receive the same per capita resourcing. However, they differ widely in learning outcomes: the Western Cape performs at the top and the Eastern Cape near the bottom of the country's educational assessments. Table 5.1 gives the results of standardized tests administered in 2007 to sixth-graders by the independent Southern and East African Consortium for Monitoring Educational Quality (SACMEQ). As it

Table 5.1 Comparison of SACMEQ education scores (average mathematics and home language)

Region	50th percentile (median)	25th percentile	75th percentile
Western Cape	560	496	636
Eastern Cape	454	408	509
South Africa (overall)	495	446	579

Note: achievement in grade 6 mathematics and home language by province, 2007.
Source: authors' calculations, from SACMEQ data files (2007); RSA, DBE (2010).

shows, whether we look at learners in the 25th, 50th, or 75th percentile in their province, the Western Cape clearly outperforms the South Africa average, and further outstrips the Eastern Cape by an even larger margin.

Our research found that the character of the subnational political settlements in the two provinces played a major role in explaining this variance. While the African National Congress (ANC) has dominated national elections since 1994, both provinces feature significant province-level political contestation within this national picture of dominance. The Western Cape has tended, since 1994, to experience robust party-political competition, with seven different political parties or coalitions controlling the province during this period. In the Eastern Cape, by contrast, the ANC superficially appears to enjoy dominance, never receiving less than 70 per cent of the vote since 1994. However, this masks endemic inter-elite conflict under the umbrella of the ANC, stemming from the social base of the settlement in the Eastern Cape, an attempt to stitch together former Bantustans with the old Cape Provincial Administration.

Thus, the political settlements in both provinces feature significant factionalism, albeit in quite different ways. The real difference comes in the institutional character within the settlements. The Western Cape inherited an institutional legacy in public service that had, with the rather large caveat of 'under the terms of apartheid', featured a largely 'Weberian' impersonal and rules-based character. The relative success of the education system in the Western Cape seems to a significant degree to come from continued high levels of bureaucratic capacity. In the Eastern Cape, by contrast, the two formerly independent Bantustans of Transkei and Ciskei had been organized politically around personalized, patronage interests, and integrating these two distinct polities with each other and with the former Cape Provincial Administration was a major institutional challenge. In the post-apartheid era, competing political parties have not been able convincingly and legitimately to commit to delivering new policies and performance in the education sector. By contrast, in the Western Cape, competitive pressure have interacted with bureaucratic capacity to create credible incentives for reform. The difference can therefore be substantially explained by the better performance of the relatively impersonal and hierarchical education bureaucracy in the west, buttressed by a competitive multiparty system. This is in contrast to the more personalized and politicized bureaucracy in the east, where an apparently dominant party system has in practice been subject to fragmentation and intra-elite competition (Levy et al. 2018). This suggests that institutional arrangements interact dynamically with the political settlement, and is in line with the wider finding that electoral competition can tend to exacerbate the politics of patronage, unless a longer-term process of state-building has already taken place (Grindle 2012; Fukuyama 2016, also Chapter 7).

In South Africa's Western Cape, as in Ghana and Uganda, coalitions mattered at the local as well as national level. Success in promoting learning depended on the efforts of district- and community-level coalitions coming together to offset collective action problems and devise institutional fixes in contexts where there was little system-wide pressure for imposing reforms down through the system. District-level coalitions involving politicians, bureaucrats, and sometimes teachers' associations helped devise clear systems of performance monitoring and accountability and sometimes also co-financing arrangements, in close relationship with headteachers, school management committees, parent–teacher associations, and traditional rulers. At school level, politically connecting members on school management committees often helped to improve flows of both information and resources. On the one hand, the decentralized governance arrangements in both Ghana's and Uganda's education domain have reduced the potential for system-wide pressures to be exerted effectively from national down to local levels. On the other hand, it has afforded the space for multi-stakeholder coalitions to emerge and forge some creative solutions within otherwise dysfunctional public-sector settings. These were absent in Rwanda, where there is a lack of political space within which to experiment even at local levels.

Examining the politics of social provisioning in the domain of education thus offers important insights into the different ways in which political settlements shape the capacity and commitment to deliver development. These insights flow directly from an examination of the interplay between different

Table 5.2 Indicators of elite commitment to reforms for high-quality education

Case	Level of government priority given to quality-focused education reforms	Level of policy coherence on education over time	Presence of strong technocratic lead/cadre with autonomy within education domain	Elite commitment
Unit of measure	0.5–6*	0.5–6*	0.5–6*	Aggregate score
Bangladesh	3	2	2	7
Cambodia	5	3.5	4	12.5
Ghana	2	1	2.5	5.5
Rwanda	1	1.5	2	4.5
Uganda	1	1	1	3
South Africa	2.5	3	4	9.5

* Weak: 0.5–1.5; Moderate 2–3.5; Strong 4–6.
Source: authors.

power domains, in that the politics of development plays out differently depending on the type of policy domain involved.

First, regarding political settlement types, the pressures within clientelist political settlements to make political use of this domain to secure rents and legitimacy are difficult to overcome. On the other hand, our findings challenge Khan's assumptions (2010) that dominant coalitions will tend to offer higher levels of developmental governance and the most effective pathway to improved levels of inclusive development. This is particularly where the policy challenge at hand is of a transactional rather than a logistical nature (Andrews et al. 2012). In terms of education, our findings suggest that more competitive settlements, within which there are a wider range of stakeholders actively involved in helping to monitor and improve performance, perform better on more transactional policy challenges. Moreover, it can be particularly difficult in dominant contexts to challenge the kinds of policy ideas that seem to be undermining the advance of educational quality, as observed in the cases of Rwanda and Uganda with regards to the language of instruction and populist commitment to 'free' education.

Secondly, the social configuration of power emerges as highly influential, not only in terms of the threat perceptions of ruling coalitions, but also in relation to the sociological character of different groups within the political settlement. The strength of the coalitions that helped support and that now maintain increased access to schooling (involving, for instance, populist leaders, large rural constituencies, teachers and teachers' unions, and donors) far outweighs the kind of coalition that might in time emerge in support of higher learning outcomes (involving, for example, enlightened political leaders, a sufficiently powerful capitalist class, middle-class parents, or teachers' associations).

Third, looking at education helps reveal the importance of extending a power-domains perspective to the local level, which is where most of the action to promote learning takes place. An understanding of the local configuration of power helped to explain here how developmental coalitions emerged in ways that significantly improved performance.

When Do Governments Commit to Improving the Quality of Health-service Provisioning? The Case of Maternal Mortality

In most parts of rural Africa, a woman giving birth is several hundred times more likely to die than her counterpart in most parts of the global north.[3] Even on a minimalist account of rights (e.g. Caney 2006), this fact constitutes a grievously unjust form of global inequality. The challenge of maternal health, and particularly the issue of maternal mortality, has risen to prominence since the late twentieth century, aided by its inclusion within the Millennium Development Goals (MDGs). However, progress towards targeted improvements has been highly uneven across countries, and it has been relatively rare for maternal mortality to become a political priority at national levels (Shiffman 2007). Indeed, the implementation of health-sector reforms is 'a politically infused process' (Shiffman 2007: 802), yet this topic has received relatively little scholarly attention. In our four-country study we examined to what extent efforts made in this part of the health policy domain, and attendant variations in progress in reducing maternal mortality rates (MMR), could be tracked back to political settlement dynamics, and what lessons this holds for practical efforts to reduce the MMR in different types of political context. To this end, we undertook both cross-country comparison and within-country process-tracing for Bangladesh, Ghana, Rwanda, and Uganda.

Figure 5.1 shows the MMR trajectory for 1990–2015. Bangladesh has the lowest absolute figures, but the rate of decline in Rwanda is by far the steepest. Indeed, by 2015, Rwanda had overtaken Ghana and had exceeded the fifth MDG target of reducing maternal mortality by 75 per cent. Bangladesh (69 per cent) had just missed the target, while Ghana (49 per cent), and Uganda (50 per cent) had missed it by a considerable margin (although they still performed better than the low-income country average). Importantly, these differing rates of progress cannot be simply explained in terms of the technical inputs that each country has invested in this policy domain. As set out in Table 5.3, of these countries, Ghana spends the most money per capita on health and has the highest percentage of public expenditure, closely followed by Rwanda, then Uganda, with Bangladesh the lowest spender. As a percentage of GDP, Uganda actually spends the most, and also has the highest external component to its health spending, followed by Rwanda, then Ghana, and finally Bangladesh. (Note that Ghana is considerably richer than the other countries in our sample.)

The four country case studies display a range of different political settlements: Rwandan politics features a classic 'dominant'-type settlement; Ghana, by contrast, displays a highly competitive scenario (see Table 5.4

[3] This section draws on the comparative study by Kelsall (2020) and the ESID papers synthesized therein—namely, on Ghana (Abdulai 2018), Uganda (Bukenya and Golooba-Mutebi 2019), Rwanda (Golooba-Mutebi with Habiyonizeye 2018), and Bangladesh (Mahmud with Sharmeen and Mazhab 2020).

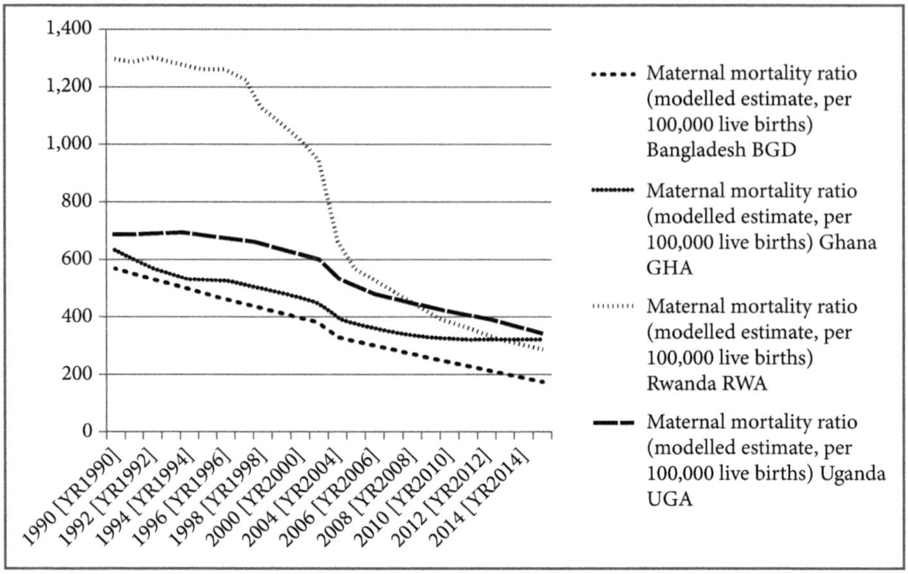

Figure 5.1 Maternal mortality trends, 1990–2015
Source: authors' calculations, from World Bank data, 17 February 2016.

for a summary of the four case studies). Uganda and Bangladesh are somewhat more complicated, with a temporal element: Uganda has arguably, since around 2000, been moving from full dominance to a scenario where the ruling regime faces considerably greater competitive threat. Bangladesh has been going in the opposite direction; it was fully competitive for most of the period under examination here, shifting towards dominance from 2009, with the Awami League consolidating its position more fully after the controversial 2014 elections. (See Appendix I, country summaries).

As such, this spread of cases offered the ability to test some hypotheses generated by the existing literature on political settlements, as discussed below. As with education, the study also had a within-country element, comparing better and worse performing districts in each country. A process-tracing methodology was used in the case studies, supplemented with cross-case and within-case comparison, to develop the synthesis conclusions given here.

Overall, we find that different types of political settlement are likely to shape different pathways towards progress on maternal health outcomes. Although there is reason to believe that dominant-type settlements are more likely to feature the conditions for effective implementation of policy compared to competitive-type settlements, this is not a simple and deterministic relationship and significant progress can also be made via a more competitive route. We looked at how progress can be made within the distinctive

Table 5.3 Health finance indicators, 2013

Country	Health expenditure per capita (US$)	Health expenditure as % GDP	External resources as % health expenditure	Annual increase in Overseas Development Assistance (ODA) for Maternity and Child Health (MNCH)	Public health expenditure as % of total	Out of pocket expenditure as % of total
Bangladesh	32	7.8	8.6	11.5	35.3	60.2
Ghana	99	10.6	13.2	11.6	60.6	36.2
Rwanda	70	22.3	38	29.5	58.8	18.4
Uganda	59	24.3	45.5	9.7	44.4	38.4
All low income	37	not available	31.7	not available	41.5	40.7

Source: authors' calculations, from World Data Bank, 17 February 2016, and Hsu (2015).

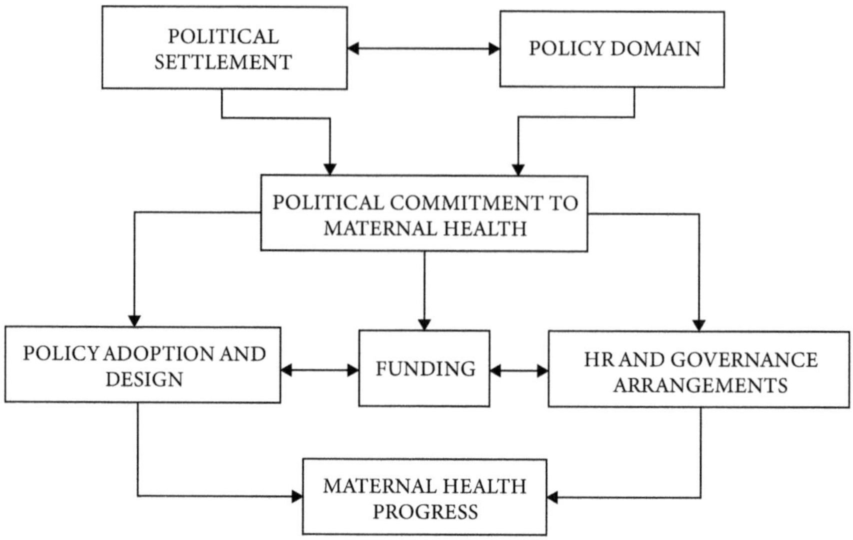

Figure 5.2 Main causal mechanisms in the politics of maternal health
Source: Kelsall (2020).

constraints and opportunities furnished by different types of political settlement. High-performing subnational jurisdictions exist even in seemingly less propitious political circumstances, such as northern Ghana. Understanding how these can be encouraged and built upon is important. Indeed, the fact that healthcare is a decentralized service in our case-study countries emerged as significant: particularly where national guidance and oversight was weak (as in all cases apart from Rwanda), local politics and governance were critical. For this reason, the subnational level is at least as important as the national here. Our results offer a further illustration of the importance of the interaction between underlying political settlements, at both national and subnational levels, and the character of the specific policy domain. We find that this interaction shapes the degree and nature of political commitment to maternal health, and, through that, policy design and choice, funding levels, and whether or not human resource and governance arrangements support effective implementation (Figure 5.2).

Rwanda: National Level

Rwanda exceeded the MDG5 target of reducing the MMR by 75 per cent. Health units are well functioning, and there has been an improvement in emergency obstetric care and an upsurge in facility births. Our analysis (see Golooba-Mutebi with Habiyonizeye (2018)) suggests that this impressive record can largely be attributed to Rwanda's dominant, developmental political settlement, which drives effective policy implementation through hierarchical performance mechanisms, as with much in contemporary Rwanda (Golooba-Mutebi with Habiyonizeye 2011).

Strong top-down accountability measures are clearly evident in health: performance contracts run through the system, down from the president through local mayors and local health officials, right through to community health workers, who in turn encourage expectant mothers to seek antenatal care and to have facility births. Local officials are aware that good performance will advance their careers (or bad performance vice versa). Strict reporting requirements ensure that health indicators are regularly monitored and localities ranked in local or national performance, and a spirit of competition among districts is fostered. There are regular inspections of facilities. There are also significant bottom-up accountability measures. Local citizens are represented on health centre management committees, and the fact that most Rwandans are enrolled in the public health system through community health insurance encourages ordinary citizens to voice their concerns.

The explanation for many of these outcomes can be traced back to features of the political settlement, such as the legitimation strategy seen as necessary by the RPF, core ideas embedded in the post-conflict moment, and the near-absence of competitive pressures. The ruling coalition is wary of the risk of being perceived to be a minority Tutsi regime ruling a majority Hutu population in an ethnically partial manner and has eschewed patronage handouts to particular groups and instead staked its legitimacy on delivering broad-based economic and social development. This has included trying to improve the position and well-being of women in Rwandan society. A commitment to women's rights and physical security is a core legitimating idea of the regime, stemming from the horrors visited upon women in the civil war and genocide (Burnet and d'Arc Kanakuze 2018: 49). This is a further factor predisposing the country to good performance on maternal health. Finally, the RPF's current dominance acts as an enabling factor insofar as that the common temptations of competition—such as distributing resources to serve political ends, rather than development goals or need, and tacitly allowing corruption—are avoided, and, in implementation, local-level actors are subject to univocal top-down control that brooks no deviation.

Ghana: National Level

Ghana, by contrast, has the worst record within our sample. This is despite Ghana being the most democratic and the wealthiest country of the four, and despite the fact that maternal health is seemingly not a politically marginal issue, with strong rhetorical commitments from both major parties and many action plans. Here we found that the competitive political settlement was key; under constant threat of losing power, recent Ghanaian governments have tended to favour highly visible short-term infrastructure projects that can be trumpeted to voters, instead of less obvious system improvements, and are loathe to provoke the ire of powerful interest groups such as doctors, who often obstruct attempts to manage personnel more effectively. This scenario also encourages undisciplined public-sector expansion and populist policy-making, as well as frequent discontinuities in policy, organization, and key leadership positions (as discussed in Chapter 6).

For instance, there were seven different Ministers of Health in Ghana between 2009 and 2015. Rewards and sanctions theoretically involved in the performance management system are rarely enforced. A regional health director commented in interview: 'Have I ever been called and asked: Director, this is your contract with me, what have you done? No! There is no follow through. You sign, and you take pictures, and they sign, but then what else? Nothing!' (Abdulai 2018: 19). Although there are comparatively high numbers of trained health staff in the country, absenteeism and poor distribution of staff across districts are both problems. Moreover, although the health sector is predominantly publically financed, the budget is dominated by staff salaries: in 2013, 98 per cent of government allocations to the ministry were taken up with staff salaries (Ghana MoH 2015), with the effect that the sector remains reliant on donor funds for capital expenditures. In light of this context, it is perhaps not surprising that Ghana missed the MDG5 target by some way, achieving only a 49 per cent reduction in the MMR. Overall, we found no evidence of any systematic drive at national level to improve performance throughout the health domain, although, as discussed below, some regions manage to buck the national trend.

Uganda: National Level

The Ugandan case compares instructively with Ghana, in that the country's shift away from a dominant to a more competitive political settlement from around 2001 has undermined Uganda's health-sector performance in ways that mirror the problems encountered in Ghana. During the period of dominance in the 1990s, technocrats were appointed to the health ministry and largely allowed to perform their role with political support, with, for instance, good performance in the area of HIV/AIDS (Putzel 2004). However, this changed once the ruling coalition became more vulnerable to challenges from the early 2000s, a shift that strengthened incentives to use the sector as a source of patronage. High-performing officials in the Ministry of Health were replaced by associates of President Museveni: successive high-level corruption scandals ensued, and performance declined. Uganda too fell significantly short of MDG5, with a reduction in the MMR of only 50 per cent. The policy framework can be considered technically sound, with well-identified priorities in emergency obstetric care, increased access to skilled attendants at birth, family planning, and antenatal care to prevent diseases responsible as indirect causes of maternal deaths (Bukenya and Golooba-Mutebi 2019: 6–7). However, there are major implementation problems in the system, with bottlenecks in medical supplies and infrastructure, poor coordination, and a general shortage of both financial and human resources. These issues have been exacerbated by the phenomenon of 'districtization', in which the central regime has succumbed to the temptation to create irrationally large numbers of new districts in order to generate political positions to distribute as patronage, leading to the hurried creation of new district health authorities. Additionally, as in Ghana, rapid turnover in senior health officials, appointed and removed in a politicized fashion, militates against consistency and long-termism. Thus, in Uganda, the longitudinal shift in the nature of the political settlement emerges as a key explanatory factor of national-level trends, with dynamics generated by this shift stymieing performance in the health sector.

A final, complicated factor is the role of foreign actors. The MMR figures appear to suggest that, around the time when competitive pressures and related clientelism were really beginning to bite in Uganda's health sector (*c*.2004–6), there was a counter-intuitive marginal acceleration in the reduction in the MMR. Explaining this would require further research, but it seems likely that donor resources have been crucial in enhancing the health sector's delivery capacity and may have patched over problems. However, key figures in Ugandan health also consider that donors have wielded excessive influence over decision-making, which, coupled with their proclivity for establishing their own pet implementation structures, has further undermined collective action in the health domain (Bukenya and Golooba-Mutebi 2019).

Bangladesh: National Level

Bangladesh suggests an alternative pathway towards improved performance in the health sector. The country has progressed more rapidly than either Ghana or Uganda over the same time frame and achieved the best outcomes (in absolute figures for MMR) of any country in our sample, albeit from a stronger starting point. This seems surprising, given that Bandladesh's public-health sector is dysfunctional in many ways, as expected within a competitive–clientelist type of political settlement. Nonetheless, a mixture of paradigmatic elite-level commitment to social provisioning and the presence of a strong civil society has produced some impressive results, albeit within the context of Bangladesh narrowly missing the MDG5 target, with a 69 per cent reduction in the MMR.

Bangladesh experiences many similar problems to those of Ghana and Uganda. While maternal health has been fairly high on the political agenda for some time, there has been a bias towards conspicuous infrastructure rather than performance, as well as poor distribution and disciplining of staff. The pressures of competitive politics have left central government unwilling or unable to impose its will on other interest groups and centres of power. As in Ghana, doctors exert considerable influence as a professional group, and the government is reluctant to irk them; senior practitioners' and doctors' associations have successfully resisted several human-resources initiatives. There is also conflict of interest between two different agencies responsible for implementation of maternal health policy (Mahmud with Sharmeen and Mahzab 2020).

Thus, it is perhaps surprising that the MMR has declined as fast as it has in Bangladesh. It is possible that contextual development factors such as women's education and better nutrition, areas in which Bangladesh has made significant progress, are relevant. There is also comparatively high-quality private obstetric care, partly indicated by Bangladesh's very high level of out-of-pocket health expenditure, and the private sector probably compensates for some of the inadequacies of the public sector (with damaging implications for cost and equity). In particular, it is likely that a key factor explaining this puzzle is the major involvement of non-governmental actors within the health domain, particularly at local levels, including NGO programmes in areas such as community health, family planning, and obstetric care (Ahmed et al. 2013). This is important to our overall theoretical findings: it suggests that a political settlements approach can help identify the different pathways that are available for achieving improved development outcomes within the context of specific configurations of power, rather than only explaining absolute levels of outcome (Figure 5.3). This ability to explain equifinality can help policy actors to identify the kinds of interventions that will 'fit' with particular types of context (see Chapter 7).

Country	Political settlement	Progress on maternal health	Key causal factors
Rwanda	*Dominant*	Strong. Exceeded MDG5 target of 75% reduction in MMR. Sector functions well.	• Central regime's unified developmental vision and problem-solving approach, and lack of electoral political threats. • Strong top-down accountability mechanisms. • Ideational importance of women's rights to the government's legitimacy.
Uganda	*(Decreasingly) Dominant*	Mixed. Missed MDG5 (only 50% reduction). However, wide local variation, with some pockets of effectiveness. Also, rate of decline in MMR may have accelerated, for reasons currently unclear.	• Increased political competition has fostered damaging patronage effects. • Related rapid creation of new districts has destabilized service provision. • However, where decentralized authorities enjoy clement local political conditions (unified, clear vision, useful connections to power), good performance can emerge
Ghana	*Competitive*	Limited. Missed MDG5 (only 49% reduction). Much political discourse, but disappointing results. Good numbers of personnel, but poorly distributed. Local pockets of effectiveness.	• Politicization of health sector and related effects: ▪ appointment by fiat and frequent turnover; policy discontinuity; ▪ powerful interest groups (especially doctors) and related government reluctance to enforce performance sanctions against endemic absenteeism; ▪ tendency towards short-termist and highly visible infrastructure projects over system improvement. • Pocket of effectiveness in Upper East, one of the country's most impoverished areas, driven by visionary leadership with strong oversight mechanisms.
Bangladesh	*(Decreasingly) Competitive*	Mixed. Missed MDG5 fairly narrowly (69% reduction). Problems with performance and geographical distribution of staff. However, relatively rapid reduction in MMR.	• Central government reluctant, given electoral pressures, to challenge powerful interest groups such as doctors' associations. • Politicization of implementing agencies, which are sometimes in competition regarding their overlapping mandates. • Problems in distribution of staff and resources, especially to remote locations. • NGOs are politically influential and may well be playing a significant role in contributing to the health sector's performance on maternal health.

Figure 5.3 Maternal health case studies summary
Source: authors, drawing from Kelsall (2020)

The Subnational Level

The study also looked at comparatively higher-performing and lower-performing districts in each country. It is worth beginning by noting the unusual case here. In Rwanda, such is the consistency of high performance across districts, the actual differences in outcomes were not especially great, and our study had difficulty establishing compelling causal explanations for the difference. This in itself is an illuminating illustration of the Rwandan context, which, as above, features an unusually high level of top-down control and performance and accountability measures, and demonstrates the workings of an integrated system. However, this is unusual, both within our cases and in the wider world. Thus, a national-level analysis can take us only so far with regards to a form of social provisioning that is decentralized and intensely local in nature, with the quality of the service often defined through the interaction of frontline service providers and citizens. Our within-country comparative case-study analyses explored the interaction between local-level configurations of power and institutional performance on maternal mortality. The local units of governance and social contexts of the 'good' and 'bad' performers were otherwise comparable in terms of ethnic composition, socio-economic status, and so on. (In the Ghana case, even more revealingly, the worse-performing area was located in a comparatively affluent context whereas the better-performing area was in a notoriously impoverished context.) The results were striking and revealed the importance of taking our power-domains analysis down to the local level.

In Uganda, we compared two neighbouring districts that presented markedly different pictures in maternal health provision. In Uganda's annual health-sector performance reports, between 2007 and 2014, Sembabule consistently featured in the bottom fifteen districts, whereas Lyantonde was always in the top fifteen.[4] The two are neighbouring districts, and share similar sociocultural and economic contexts. In terms of maternal health specifically, Sembabule had only 11.4 per cent of deliveries take place in health facilities in 2013/14, ranking it 107th; Lyantonde achieved 74.4 per cent and has been ranked as high as fourth. In Sembabule, the district Health Centre is dilapidated and unsanitary (Bukenya and Golooba-Mutebi 2019: 16). A lack of anaesthetists and blood-transfusion equipment means that the centre does not carry out caesarean sections, ordinarily a central component of emergency obstetrics. In theory, where there is a lack of ability to

[4] As of 2020 there are 134 districts in Uganda, but this number has changed considerably (upwards) over recent years (as mentioned above, a major political issue in its own right). The important point for this discussion is that the two districts are typically towards the bottom and top of the rankings respectively.

deal with complicated pregnancies, patients can receive emergency referral to higher-level or neighbouring facilities. However, in Sembabule all ambulances have been grounded for years, and there is no referral system. Given these issues, it is common for women—especially of poorer families—to seek the care of (now illegal) traditional birth attendants instead. While such figures are valued by some for stepping into gaps in state provision, this is nevertheless associated with higher numbers of avoidable maternal deaths. In Lyantonde, by contrast, the health infrastructure is comparatively well developed and maintained. The maternity and women's wards were hygienic and organized, albeit stretched by high numbers. The referral system is in place, with ambulances to facilitate it. The management team regularly monitors data to assess progress against targets, and in general the district has a relatively well-functioning monitoring and evaluation framework.

Thus, we have an intriguing picture of two neighbouring districts, alike in many contextual aspects, with dramatically differing performance in maternal health. We found that there is a clear political explanation for this. Within a national context featuring weak dominance at the centre, and quite thoroughgoing decentralization of service provision, local-level configurations of power—what we could call 'local political settlements'—and how these interacted with national-level political settlement dynamics, became particularly salient. In low-performing Sembabule, local politics is characterized by intensely factional and debilitating conflict between two politicians, each with national profiles and close connections to the president, who appears unwilling or unable to discipline them. This has created a stalemate at the district headquarters, where between 2006 and 2010 the district could not recruit, confirm, promote, or retire health staff, and performance-based accountability has been replaced by politicized shielding. In contrast, local elites in Lyantonde have formed a 'developmental coalition' around the goal of better service delivery and development, which involves politicians, bureaucrats, leading 'sons of the soil', and traditional leaders. This coalition makes adroit use of personal connections to lobby hard at national level for improvements to health infrastructure; one of the district's two MPs is a minister for health, while the national permanent secretary in health is also from the area. The political leadership also works with technical staff in a symbiotic way, and performance monitoring is strict. As one health worker explained: 'We the health workers deliver the services and they take the credit. In return, they help us to mobilise communities and get the materials and equipment we need to deliver' (Bukenya and Golooba-Mutebi 2019: 28). The district leadership has been proactive, in terms of both devising top-down oversight mechanisms and seeking out support from non-governmental actors. There is some degree of community feedback, such as through free telephone hotlines.

In Ghana, surprisingly, one of the best performers on maternal mortality during the 2010s has been Upper East Region (UER), long one of the most impoverished areas of the country (21.3 per cent extreme poverty, compared to 8.4 per cent nationally), with one of the worst doctor–population ratios (in 2013, 27,391, compared to a national average of 9,749). In the years 2011–13, Upper East recorded the highest figures for antenatal visits and skilled deliveries in Ghana, and its postnatal care coverage was significantly above the national average, and its MMR significantly below. By contrast, Volta Region (VR) is comparatively affluent and enjoys above-average health infrastructure. It has, for instance, better ambulance coverage than Upper East, and a considerably better doctor-to-population ratio (although still above the national average of one doctor for 20,625 people). Yet, its performance on health indicators in general and on maternal health in particular stands out as being very poor in national comparison (Table 5.4). Thus, there is a case of counter-intuitive subnational variation.

Our research found that most of the improvements in Upper East Region can be attributed to the creation of a pocket of effectiveness under the dynamic leadership of the regional director for health, who inspired others with his vision and conduct. Since 2008, performance has improved rapidly through a mixture of sticks (regular inspections and audits) and carrots (improved living quarters for staff in remote areas, prize-giving and awards for good performance). Monitoring and accountability are strong and are felt right down to lowest-level staff, with regular visits from seniors, letters of commendation publicly lauding well-performing individuals, and meetings for local managers at which the performances of districts are compared, fostering a degree of healthy competition. There have also been important innovations in human resources. The region has addressed its erstwhile

Table 5.4 Selected maternal health indicators, 2011–2013

Years	Skilled delivery rate			MMR			Antenatal 4+ visits			Postnatal care coverage (%)		
Area	UER	VR	Ghana	UER	VR	Ghana	UER	VR	Ghana	UER	VR	Ghana
2011	64.6	40.8	49.1	127	201	174	92.1	74.0	75.2	78.7	58.2	65.3
2012	68.6	44.9	55.0	136	174	152	94.5	74.3	77.0	77.0	53.4	62.7
2013	67.5	43.4	55.3	108	161	155	87.5	67.7	72.6	76.6	55.1	64.1

Source: authors' calculations, from Ministry of Health (MoH) 2013 and 2014 annual review reports; antenatal care visits from Ghana Health Service (GHS) (2014: 11). (Table copied from Abdulai 2018.)

'hardship-post' status through measures such as providing attractive living quarters in remote areas, introducing a 'bond' system making it mandatory for staff trained in the area to remain for three years, and in general cultivating an awareness that genuinely good performance in Upper East will be recognized with the opportunity to move on elsewhere. Ideas also matter here: all health staff are aware that the regional director treats every maternal death as a preventable tragedy and are motivated accordingly. In Volta, by contrast, monitoring mechanisms are not strongly adhered to. Given a lack of effective field visits, much monitoring is dependent on self-completed forms by local officials. In general, poor supervision of lower-level health facilities appears central to understanding the surprisingly poor performance of the Volta Region in maternal health (Abdulai 2018). Upper East also saw significant improvement on the issue of transport for emergency referrals, with an innovative repurposing of the widespread 'motor king' vehicles, supported by donors. The scheme was subsequently expanded to national roll-out, in an example of innovation in a local-level pocket of effectiveness feeding into the national level. Overall, then, a subnational perspective was critical in shedding light on why district- and regional-level performance varied so greatly, and in identifying potential pathways towards better progress (Abdulai 2018).

In Bangladesh, the two subdistricts (*upazilas*) we compared—higher-performing Patuakhali Sadar and lower-performing Kamalganj—are within districts (Patuakhali and Moulvibazar, respectively) with similar economic characteristics and poverty rates. In 2012, Kamalganj had markedly worse mortality rates, in all of the categories of maternal (24, compared to 3 in Patuakhali Sadar), neonatal (16.96 per 1,000 compared to 0.88), infant (20.69 per 1,000 compared to 2.36, and child (1–5 years) (25.67 compared to 5.89). Although, as mentioned earlier, it seems likely that the role of NGOs is important to Bangladesh's relatively good progress on reducing the MMR, in these two subdistricts there are no NGO clinics—so that rules out one factor that might possibly have explained the difference.

Our research found a complicated picture (Mahmud with Sharmeen and Mahzab 2020). One possible factor is social context: Kamalganj appeared to be an area with somewhat more religiously conservative and traditional practices, with a preference for higher family sizes, home delivery with traditional birth attendants, and cultural barriers that prevented women from seeking routine antenatal care. By contrast, in Patuakhali Sadar there seemed greater acceptance of modern services, trained birth attendants, family planning, and antenatal care. As in the local cases in Ghana, monitoring and supervision also appeared to be an important differentiating factor. In Kamalganj, supervision at the community level is sporadic and uncoordinated, whereas in Patuakhali Sadar local clinics are regularly visited by seniors, and there are monthly monitoring meetings for health field staff. However, absenteeism of staff is a significant problem in both subdistricts. Some of these monitoring problems stem from a lack of coordination between the government bodies responsible for, respectively, health and family planning, whose politicized competition and hostility is a national-level feature. In Patuakhali Sadar, however, this did not seem to be a problem; possibly it had been overcome by the fact that local-level staff were generally recruited directly from the local community, smoothing relations. Finally, political factors are relevant, particularly in terms of the relationship between local leaders and the MP. Our research found that, perhaps somewhat counter-intuitively, the absenteeism of the MP in Patuakhali Sadar (a high-ranking opposition party figure who was often away in the capital) allowed the subdistrict chairman and local mayor a degree of space to operate, and they appeared to have a genuine dedication to improving outcomes. By contrast, in Kamalganj, the MP was an influential government minister who enjoyed great popularity in the local area and prided himself on being hands-on there. The subdistrict chairman was from an opposition party, and the lack of coordination between him and the MP—and the latter's overbearing influence—made it hard for the subdistrict chairman to perform his role, with adverse effects on the health system.

Our findings show how political settlement dynamics directly affect both national and local-level performance in the health sector. To some extent they offer further support to previous work that has suggested that, in general, 'dominant-developmental' settlements (as in Rwanda) are more likely to be able to design and implement effective policies in service provision (Levy and Walton 2013). However, this is not a simple and deterministic relationship. First, as we found in other areas, political commitment to deliver progress on maternal health appears to be shaped by the interaction of the political settlement with the more contingent variables of actors, ideas, and interest groups in a particular policy domain. For example, Bangladesh has made impressive progress on maternal mortality not through top-down enforcement mechanisms through the public sector but through a loose alliance with high-capacity civil society organizations. Secondly, both progress and dysfunction in health provision can exist in both dominant and competitive scenarios: the more important question is to understand the distinctive constraints and opportunities furnished by different types of political settlements. In a dominant-developmental scenario, as in Rwanda, a 'government-supporting' strategy for development partners, predominantly just getting behind the ruling coalition's efforts, appears likely to optimize results. In scenarios where intense politicized competition is breeding dysfunction, development partners may be better advised to work on narrower issue areas, or at subnational levels, and to build 'multi-stakeholder coalitions' (Levy 2014) involving state, private, civil society, and NGO actors to try to create or support pockets of effectiveness.

6

The Politics of Governance and State Capacity

The question of what role the state should play in delivering development, and what type of state is best suited to this role, has long been at the heart of discussions around the politics of development for academic and policy actors alike. The answer to this puzzle has varied considerably over time and has been as strongly informed by ideological preference as by the evidence, as famously revealed in the World Bank's struggle to assert a market-led interpretation of the Asian success stories as against a more developmentalist state reading (Wade 1996). The mainstream response, from the 1990s until at least the late 2000s, was defined by the 'good-governance' agenda (see Chapter 1). Backed by debt-based conditionality, this involved a concerted effort to reform the state in developing countries in line with liberal principles of democracy and governance and in direct support of a neoliberal policy agenda (Harrison 2010). However, and as discussed in Chapter 1, the clash between these normative ideals and political realities in developing countries was a fairly painful one. By the end of the 2000s, even those development agencies that had conceived and led the good-governance agenda conceded that it had performed at best partially (World Bank 2008; DFID 2011). Since around 2010, the search has been on for a more realistic governance agenda, involving a shift away from widespread public-sector reform programmes to more problem-solving initiatives, and including a growing focus on the role that specific pockets of bureaucratic effectiveness (PoEs) might play in delivering development.

This chapter proceeds by first summarizing our research into the politics of public-sector reforms in Africa during the 2000s, with case-study evidence drawn from Ghana, Rwanda, and Uganda, before turning to a five-country study of PoEs in Africa, with Kenya and Zambia as the additional countries involved here. The conclusion returns to the importance of analysing current patterns of governance in Africa from a political settlements perspective that takes both ideological and transnational influences seriously, and to the

Pathways to Development. Sam Hickey and Kunal Sen, Oxford University Press.
 DOI: 10.1093/oso/9780198872566.003.0006

ongoing tensions within both development theory and practice concerning the balance between concerns over inclusion and effectiveness.

What Explains the Wide Variation in the Success of Public-sector Reform across African Countries?

The public sector remains pivotal to countries' development prospects.[1] Yet, despite both strong international support and domestic expressions of political commitment, the public-sector reform (PSR) agenda has seen, across the African continent, widely varying outcomes; some limited successes, and a variety of disappointments (World Bank 2008). The Worldwide Governance Indicators suggest that between 1996 and 2014, a period that coincides closely with major international efforts to promote 'good governance', Africa not only trailed every other region for 'Government Effectiveness' and 'Control of Corruption', but actually, on average, regressed on these measures.

The literature has typically offered two (related) explanations for the failures of PSR and state-building more generally across Africa.

The first points to historical legacies. In the mid-twentieth century, newly independent African states found themselves putatively governing territories that, in reality, had no history of effective territory-based state control, either in the precolonial era, or under colonial authorities, who typically limited state-building to capital cities and chosen sectors (Herbst 2000). Despite gaining international recognition, such states were significantly lacking in actual empirical statehood (Jackson and Rosberg 1982; Jackson 1993).

The second standard explanation is institutional mismatch. Postcolonial African states came to feature a 'neopatrimonial' blend: the formal trappings of impersonal bureaucracy, combined with an underlying continuation of personalistic forms of political authority that viewed the state as a prize whose spoils could be used to service clientelist relationships (Médard 1982; Callaghy and Ravenhill 1993; Reno 1995). Under pressure from structural adjustment programmes, and desirous of donor money, such regimes became adept at performing a facade of reform and institutional 'best practices', while leaving the underlying patrimonial game intact (van de Walle 2001; Andrews 2013; Pritchett et al. 2013).

[1] ESID's research on public-sector performance was led by Pablo Yanguas Gil, with Abdul-Gafaru Abdulai and Daniel Appiah in Ghana, Benjamin Chemouni in Rwanda, and Badru Bukenya and William Muhumza in Uganda.

However, while there is much to be said for the historical–institutionalist explanation of the broad trends, it also has significant limits. In particular, it does not help to explain a number of important variations: between-country variations, variations within particular public sectors (including why certain agencies perform very well in otherwise difficult governance contexts, the phenomenon of 'pockets of effectiveness' (POEs) discussed below), variations between different subnational levels of government, and variation over time in ongoing dynamic processes of change. It also tends to assume a rational-actor model, militating against an appreciation of the role that ideas, rather than only utility-maximizing 'incentives', play in shaping political behaviour and in undergirding institutions (Schmidt 2008; Levi and Sacks 2009; Blyth 2010).

The power domains framework outlined in Chapter 2 allows us to move beyond these limitations. Understanding PSR as a policy domain, conditioned by the political settlement, we compared the reform processes in Ghana, Rwanda, and Uganda during the period 2000–15 (see Appiah and Abdulai 2017; Bukenya and Muhumuza 2017; Chemouni 2017; and a synthesis paper, Yanguas 2017). Some of these processes had their basis in precursors beginning from, respectively, post-civil war state-building in Uganda from 1986, the 1992 constitution and return of civilian government in Ghana, and post-genocide state-building in Rwanda from 1994. But it is particularly in the period from around 2000 that a prominent PSR agenda can be identified.

Our research looked at PSR implemented at the 'centre of government'. Such core functions can be conceptualized as falling under either 'management'—the capacity to plan, regulate, and oversee the administrative activities of the public sector in order to achieve policy goals—or 'compliance', the capacity to ensure adherence to management orders and to norms of public service that have been established, and to identify and sanction any deviations from this. The hallmark of success in PSR would, then, be increases in these capacities. Within the 'management' area, broadly three categories of reform took place: reforms targeting public sector coordination, public financial management, and public/civil service management. Within the 'compliance' area, broadly two categories of reform took place: reforms aiming to improve anti-corruption, and auditing (see Figure 6.1). In each country, the president has considerable influence over PSR (although in different ways and with different countervailing forces), as does the ministry of finance. Donors such as the World Bank and DFID-UK too have been influential in our countries, albeit with varying results.

		Ghana	Rwanda	Uganda
Management reforms	*Coordination*	National Development Planning Commission mandated by 1992 Constitution; subsequent governments each created their own separate central policy units.	The 'Vision 2020' document (2000), with its attendant Economic Development and Poverty Reduction Strategies, provides a single basis for all planning. Ministry plans reviewed by the Ministry of Finance and Prime Minister's Office.	2003 coordination framework legally places coordination with the Office of the Prime Minister. However, a plethora of bodies with overlapping claims to responsibility for coordination remains.
	Financial management	2003 public procurement Act, theoretically favouring competitive tendering. 2016 new public financial management Act legislates sanctions for irregularities in procurement. Some input of wider society in budgeting.	2006 Organic Budget Law laid the basis of modern budgeting system, and spurred training for staff. 2013 revamp integrated planning and budgeting more. In procurement: National Tender Board established 1997. 2004 Presidential order updated this, before 2007 reform decentralized most powers to public organizations.	New technology in financial management—e.g. an integrated system containing information across procurement, budgeting, and accounting for most of central government (2004). New legislation on planning and budgeting is in line with international standards.
	Public/civil service management	Freeze on recruitment since 2009. Performance agreement contracts for chief directors (re)introduced in 2013.	Public Service Commission set up 2007 to oversee fair recruitment, along with Ombudsman. 2014 reform phased out most contract-based work (previously a loophole for nepotism).	Between 2005/6and 2010/11 the Public Sector Reform Programme introduced 'results-oriented management', performance contracts, and other incentive and sanction structures, as well as attempting improvements in HR, skills, and recruitment.
Compliance reforms	*Anti-corruption*	Whistleblower Act (2006) encouraging public to report corruption. National Anti-Corruption Action Plan (2011).	Office of the Ombudsman (2003), based on Swedish model, has important anticorruption functions. Reforms in 2009 and 2013 extended powers of policing and prosecution. National Anti-Corruption Advisory Council created 2008.	Establishment of anti-corruption court (2010), strengthening of the Inspectorate of Government.
	Auditing	2003 reform created central audit agency and mandated internal audit units for public agencies. 2016 legislation update attempts to address problems of self-auditing.	Office of Auditor General created 1998, enshrined in 2003 constitution. Independence bolstered by 2013 law. The important Public Account Committee was created in 2011.	Audit Act 2008. HR innovations in the Office of the Auditor General to try to improve performance. Sectoral Audit Committees established (advisory only).
Key domestic actors		Two competing political parties (NDC and NPP). The President is afforded great power over appointments of senior bureaucrats and creation of policy units. Attorney general is also Minister of Justice and so has a high level of power in the area of compliance. Civil society anti-corruption campaigns beginning to be influential around 2016.	President Kagame and RPF inner circle. Ministry of Finance is influential in many areas and may have some sway over Auditor General via oversight of its budget. The public Urugwiro dialogues of 1998–9 (part of the extended peace process) were germinal to many subsequent developments.	President Museveni and NRM inner circle are dominant domestically and are happy to maintain the somewhat haphazard structure of agencies,since itaids control over government business. Among state agencies, Ministry of Finance is particularly powerful.
Donor influence		World Bank (around 2003 reforms). IMF (via 2015/16 loan). DFID-UK (supported one instance of presidential creation of pet central policy unit).	World Bank and DFID supported late 1990s budgeting reforms. World Bank particularly influential on high importance attached to financial management from 2000s. Auditor General supported by Swiss, Dutch, UK.	World Bank, DFID-UK, Denmark, Irish Aid, Austria funded Public Sector Reform Programme (2005/6–2010/11) via 'sector-wide approach' common pool.

Figure 6.1 Key instances of public-sector reform in Ghana, Rwanda, and Uganda, 2000–2015

Source: authors.

Thus, these three African nations, with a legacy of informalism in politics and a period of PSR between 2000 and 2015, influenced considerably by donors, share enough in common to be viable comparators. At the same time, they usefully display different political settlement dynamics. Overall, the research found that these dynamics go a long way towards explaining the varying extents to which PSR did or did not result in genuinely increased effectiveness in management and compliance. In Ghana, the competitive–clientelist political settlement has generated a situation where the bodies responsible for public-sector performance are regularly created and dissolved with every turnover of power, engendering organizational proliferation and competition, and much policy discontinuity. Donors underestimated the importance of this problem, and arguably exacerbated it on occasion. In Rwanda, the dominant political settlement has afforded the Rwandan Patriotic Front (RPF) a sense of long time-horizons that is propitious for unflashy but effective reforms, and the dominance to drive and enforce these, with donors in a largely harmonious supporting role. In Uganda, increasing threats to a once-dominant regime have seen initial acquiescence to donor-pushed reforms, and attendant legislative progress, degenerate into a major implementation gap as the clientelist politics of regime survival has eroded both management and compliance. However, the layout of power in the political settlement does not by itself offer a full explanation of these cases, with the role of ideas and the transnational influence represented by donors both also important.

Ghana

Ghana has struggled with public-sector performance since independence, a problem that improved little under the World Bank- and IMF-influenced structural adjustment reforms of the 1990s. On coming to power in 2001, the New Patriotic Party (NPP) trumpeted PSR as a major priority: it introduced a wave of World Bank-sponsored reforms to central institutions in 2003 and established a Ministry of Public Sector Reform in 2005. This was followed by a change of direction to a more sector-based approach under the National Democratic Congress (NDC) on its return to power in 2009. That year also marked the start of an IMF economic reform package whose conditionalities have been influential upon PSR.

However, the defining features of Ghana's PSR process remain fragmentation and discontinuity, which our research identifies as flowing directly from the country's highly competitive political settlement (see Appendix I, country summaries).

In the area of management, there has been a proliferation of bodies established to implement and monitor public policy, with incoming governments often setting up new units, staffed with loyal figures, and phasing out those established under their opponents. The new Policy Delivery Unit introduced under President Mahama in 2014, sponsored by DFID-UK, was the third such entity created in thirteen years. Such units duplicate—or usurp—the intended function of the constitutionally mandated National Development Planning Commission. The commission itself has also not remained immune to politicization, with governments exerting control over appointments, and switching out personnel from previous administrations, eroding any possibility of longer-term institutional learning and planning. Similarly, reforms are often stalled by electoral turnovers. For instance, the implementation of performance contracts for high-ranking civil servants in 2000 never happened owing to civil-service fears of partisan witch-hunts following the change of government in 2001.

An enabling factor to this is that, under Ghana's 1992 constitution, the president has unusually extensive power over appointments of senior public-service figures. The membership of the procurement board is also politically appointed, which allows a system whereby competitive tendering (theoretically the default mode) rarely takes place, and instead sole-source tenders are used to reward party loyalists, who in turn contribute kickbacks to the party. IMF conditions triggered a new Public Procurement Bill, passed in 2016, where parliament voted unanimously to raise procurement thresholds. However, it also presented an opportunity for MPs to vote to shift towards a politically independent procurement board. The fact that both major parties did not do so strongly underlines that, in an environment of intense competition, it is simply too tempting to maintain avenues for distributing patronage.

In this context, efforts to enforce compliance and reduce corruption struggle to get off the ground. While an independent auditor-general watches oversees agencies, responsibility for implementation of its recommendations falls to committees headed by figures from the very agencies in question, 'asking them to punish themselves' (Appiah and Abdulai 2017: 22)—with the predictable outcome that the capacity of the auditing system to hold public agencies accountable is severely undermined. Meanwhile, the decision to prosecute for corruption offences remains with the attorney general—again, a political appointee—ensuring that anti-corruption essentially becomes part-partisan strategy, part-damage control for the government of the day.

Thus, while problems with compliance and politicization might hypothetically be addressable by Ghana's public-sector institutions, these are stymied by fragmentation and policy discontinuity, which in turn result from the highly unstable and partisan competition characterizing the country's current political settlement. These factors have meant that, despite considerable expenditure and support, the interventions of donors such as Canada, the United Kingdom, and the World Bank have made little impact upon management and compliance bodies in the public sector, which remain only weakly effective, as well as highly vulnerable to subversion for clientelist ends. Indeed, the latter danger was probably insufficiently appreciated by donors, leading to a strategy ill-fitted to the distinctive context furnished by Ghana's political settlement. Donors have typically managed to do little more than support the reform flavour of the day. Where they proposed policies consistent with prevailing partisan or clientelist goals—such as new delivery units under the presidency, or raising procurement thresholds—donors gained more traction, but the aforementioned problems have limited any possible positive impacts of such measures—in fact, the measures may have contributed further to those existing problems of politicized discontinuity and clientelism. Moreover, there often appears to be competition among donors themselves to achieve noticeable influence through discrete reform programmes that are, thus, uncoordinated with each other (Appiah and Abdulai 2017: 17).

Rwanda

In the wake of the end of the civil war and genocide in 1994, and the almost complete disintegration of the state, the RPF set about rapidly rebuilding public-sector institutions, supported by a variety of donors, including the World Bank and DFID-UK. A watershed moment was the Vision 2020 plan. Launched in 2000, it outlined a clear vision for Rwandan development and spurred frequent public-sector reforms in subsequent years. This was in response to the need for more effective state performance to meet Vision 2020 targets in areas such as poverty reduction and economic growth, crucial to the legitimation strategy of a regime that grew out of a Tutsi-based organization ruling a Hutu-majority population.[2] From this point, donors supported the government's aims, and exercised influence through advocacy. For instance, the 2007 Public Expenditure and Financial Accountability (PEFA) evaluation sponsored by the World Bank had a profound impact

[2] The sense of elite vulnerability vis-à-vis the Hutu majority helping to catalyse a genuine state-building project in Rwanda is an illustration of the social dimension of power in the political settlement (Kelsall 2018; Kelsall et al. 2022), as discussed in Chapter 2.

on the RPF's appreciation of public finance management as an aspect of legitimacy-building.

Rwanda during the 2000s was an outlier in terms of PSR progress in Africa. Certainly, much of this can be explained by the unusually dominant and wilful nature of the RPF regime, within the country's dominant political settlement (see Appendix I, country summaries). The national planning system has clear and measurable objectives, and public servants are strictly monitored. The Ministry of Finance has successfully established an effective budgeting process that incorporates feedback from line ministries to identify sectoral priorities (World Bank 2014). Processes aiming to ensure transparent and merit-based recruitment to public positions are largely followed. Compliance is high, and corruption, while present, is notably low compared to neighbouring countries. The government's declaration of zero tolerance towards corruption has successfully permeated most sectors, and convictions normally result in prison sentences (Chemouni 2017: 28).

However, the dominant shape of the political settlement does not explain entirely these relatively good PSR outcomes. The prevailing ideology within the RPF regime—which grows out of its organizational and cultural history—is distinct and coherent, promoting a perception of corruption as a heinous crime, and staking the regime's legitimacy on the realization of its development vision of an impartial, rules-based state to direct a flourishing economy. This ideational foundation has been unambiguously diffused in this policy domain, with the Vision 2020 strategy described by observers as 'the only hymn sheet' in Rwanda's public sector (Campioni and Noack 2012: 5). Crucially, assistance from international donors has involved the promotion of policy ideas that were (and/or that could convincingly be framed as) consistent with the RPF's vision and societal goals. It has also often involved supporting organizations, such as the Office of the Auditor General and the National Tendering Board, that already existed de facto to solve specific problems, before becoming de jure—rather than the inverse picture, where formal rules and structures are shallowly adopted to appease donors.

Two notes of caution are needed, however. First, it would be misguided to seek a 'Rwandan model' that can straightforwardly be exported. Lessons can be gleaned, of course, but the current Rwandan state grows out of a very singular confluence of historical and contingent factors. Secondly, the Rwandan picture is not, of course, one of unblemished success. Certain notoriously corrupt bodies, such as the traffic police, escape enforcement owing to limited capacity, and the unchallenged dominance of the RPF means that doubts over its willingness to sanction key elites remain (Bozzini 2013).

Uganda

After the NRM took power in Uganda following the end of the civil war in 1986, it attempted an overhaul of the old and corrupt public administration. In the 1980s and 1990s this process fell under the influence of the World Bank and IMF through structural adjustment. Many of the international finance institutions' policy recommendations in PSR were adopted, with some effect, but were typically followed by later reversals. Another round of reforms began in the 2000s, focused mainly on public finance and on 'results-oriented management' of public servants. These have included the Public Sector Reform Programme of 2005/6–2010/11 supported by the World Bank, DFID-UK, Denmark, Irish Aid, and Austria, and public finance management reforms supported by the World Bank. In general, PSR has featured donor funding heavily, and the World Bank, in particular, has been an influential player.

Uganda represents, in this comparison, an interesting middle-ground situation, given the political settlement's shift from full dominance in the 1990s towards a situation where the ruling party is significantly weakened both in terms of vertical power—with increased agitation within the party, as well as high-profile defections from it—and horizontal power, with increased pressure from political opposition and electoral considerations (see Appendix I, country summaries). The effects of this can be seen in how PSR has played out. Following the reforms mentioned above, much of the Ugandan public sector is, in terms of formal institutional design and legal frameworks, up to international standards—for instance, in financial management (Andrews and Bategeka 2013) and in anti-corruption (Global Integrity 2011).

The problems, then, concern the gap between 'form' and 'function' (Andrews and Bategeka 2013). Despite the best-practice legal reforms, it remains the case that many public agencies disobey procurement rules, with budgets frequently underestimating expenditures (Basheka and Sabiiti 2011; Ntayi et al. 2012; IMF 2014). Ad hoc supplementary budgets are often clearly linked to regime maintenance and electioneering (Bukenya and Muhumuza 2017: 17). Responsibility for public-sector coordination is shared between the offices of the prime minister, the president, the Ministry of Finance, and the National Planning Authority. This means a lot of scope for friction and rivalry, which, according to the Government of Uganda's own review (2013) undermines national planning and implementation. However, while this looks irrational from a PSR perspective, this untidy situation serves important political functions for the regime by enabling close control over government affairs (Bukenya and Muhumuza 2017: 10).

In the area of compliance, meanwhile, Uganda is infamously unable (or unwilling) to fight corruption (Tangri and Mwenda 2013), with evidence suggesting an increase in corruption since the mid-2000s. A core problem is the president's continued ability to appoint politically pliant individuals as heads of the relevant anti-corruption organizations. Consequently, punishment of regime figures tends to be performative and designed to appease the public, while it is also common for the anti-corruption bodies to be used by the NRM to target rival figures. While this suggests a characteristic realpolitik of regime survival, there is also an ideational aspect, with the NRM historically averse to the civil service, which is regarded as a colonial residue and treated with suspicion (Bukenya and Muhumuza 2017).

Many of these problems have grown considerably worse since the mid-2000s, a fact closely linked to the shifting dynamics in the political settlement, with a once-dominant regime facing credible threats for the first time. This has only increased usage of the public sector for buying off potential elite rivals, populist resource distributions, and targeting opponents. An underlying contributory factor here is that many reforms have been suffused with donor influence, from diagnosis to funding to design. For a dominant ruling coalition short on resources, formal compliance with donor promptings was a logical strategy, and, while the NRM enjoyed dominance, it acquiesced in the reforms up to a point. However, with the opening of political competition, the use of the public sector for politically partisan purposes has become ever more tempting and flagrant, and the fact that many of the reforms were in tension with core normative ideas of the NRM meant that, once the pragmatic case for paying lip service to them weakened, commitment all but evaporated. As such, major donor investments like the Public Sector Reform Programme (2005–6 and 2010–11) have yielded disappointing results (World Bank 2015).

Overall, then, the nature of the political settlement emerges as a key explanatory factor regarding the varied PSR experiences of these three countries. A particularly important causal mechanism within this is the perceived time-horizon of ruling coalitions, with the security enjoyed by the RPF in Rwanda facilitating a more long-term approach, while in Uganda the growth of vertical and horizontal threats to the NRM's power has spurred increased politicization and patronage in the public sector to serve immediate regime-maintenance goals; in Ghana, intense partisan competition combined with clientelism has meant elite capture during government administrations and discontinuity between them.

However, the power balance in the political settlement is not the only factor. The role of ideas paradigmatic to the ruling coalition, and how these have

Case	Worldwide Governance Indicators*	Political-settlement type	PSR experience	Explanatory factors
Ghana	CoC: −0.11 (% rank 52.88) GE −0.21 (% rank 46.15)	Competitive	Very limited progress. Institutional fragmentation and policy discontinuity.	Intensely partisan competition stemming from public sector generates short-termism and clientelist elite capture; donor influence limited to going with the grain of partisanship
Rwanda	CoC: +0.58 (% rank 71.15) GE: +0.21 (% rank 62.02)	Dominant	Comparatively successful reforms leading to coherent and largely well-performing public sector agencies, with a strong culture of oversight and accountability and only limited corruption.	Strong central control and unified ideological vision; long time-horizon of government facilitated by lack of challenge to ruling coalition; donor and transnational policy ideas were able to harmonize with ideas central to ruling coalition's vision and legitimation strategy
Uganda	CoC: −1.04 (% rank 14.42) GE: −0.61 (% rank 29.81)	Vulnerable dominant	Much 'best-practice' institutional set-up and legislation, but stymied by reality of its subsumption into the patronage machine, and by endemic corruption	Shifting dynamics in the public sector—increasing horizontal competition and weakening of regime's vertical power—reveal NRM adoptionof donor-led reforms to have been largely performative and at odds with ideas and incentives central to regime

Figure 6.2 Public-sector-reform outcomes: political settlements analysis
*2018 dataset. Control of Corruption (CoC) and Government Effectiveness (GE) measures. Scale from −2.5 (weak) to +2.5 (strong), and % rank among countries.
Source: authors.

interacted with the promptings of donors within the specific policy domain of PSR, have also strongly shaped outcomes. In Ghana, policy solutions compatible with top-down oversight and that proffered 'quick wins' have tended to gain traction. In Uganda, when the regime did not feel threatened, policy agendas made the initial step into 'international best practice'-style legislation; but the changing incentives facing the regime with the growth of political competition, plus a lingering ideational wariness of the civil service, have seen the ideal legislative picture not translate into reality and instead become stymied by patronage and corruption. In Rwanda, the ruling coalition has introduced public-sector reforms, often with considerable effectiveness, that harmonized with its ideological vision for the country. Ironically—given that Rwanda is typically seen as maintaining a rather testy arm's-length relationship with donors, whereas the PSR agenda in Ghana and Uganda was ostensibly very donor-shaped—the greatest lasting donor influence may nevertheless have been in Rwanda's PSR, thanks to the subtle introduction of policy and technical ideas that the RPF recognized as having the potential to further its aims.

The 'pockets of effectiveness' Phenomenon in Africa

> [Pockets of effectiveness (PoEs) are] public organisations that are relatively effective in providing public goods and services that the organisation is officially mandated to provide, despite operating in an environment in which effective public service delivery is not the norm.
>
> **(Roll 2014: 24)**

Why do some parts of the state in developing countries perform much better than others?[3] This enduring puzzle has recently come to the fore in intellectual and strategic debates over governance and development (Roll 2014; World Bank 2017; McDonnell 2020). Within development studies, bureaucratic 'pockets of effectiveness' (PoEs) were initially highlighted for the role that they played within developmental states (Johnson 1982; Evans 1995; Leftwich 1995). However, this focus was diminished by the turn away from the state in the 1980s, reappearing only when PoEs could be associated with a

[3] The material in this section comes from a comparative research project into PoEs coordinated by Sam Hickey, with country case-studies led by Abdul-Gafaru Abdulai and Giles Mohan (Ghana), Matt Tyce (Kenya), Benjamin Chemouni (Rwanda), Badru Bukenya, Haggai Matsiko and Sam Hickey (Uganda) and Caesar Cheelo and Marja Hinfelaar and (Zambia). See Hickey (2023a) for an edited collection based on the country summaries and the ESID website for working papers on specific case-study agencies: http://www.effective-states.org/research/pockets-of-effectiveness/.

less statist project, as with the semi-autonomous agencies created during the era of privatization and new public management reforms (Leonard 1991). The resurgent interest in state-based PoEs has been catalysed by the strong turn to politics within international development during the late 2000s(e.g. Whitfield et al. 2015) and the related search to replace the now tattered certainties of the good-governance agenda with a focus on 'thinking and working politically' (see Chapter 1).

Most analyses concur that political economy factors are central in determining whether PoEs emerge and are sustained over time (Leonard 2008; Roll 2014), with other factors such as organizational leadership, organizational culture, policy mandate and function, and international support also playing important roles. However, the tendency to view PoEs as 'islands' somehow cut adrift from a sea of patronage, and the absence of systematic comparative studies of PoEs, both undermined efforts to understand the specific political economy conditions under which this happens. In contrast to the 'islands' metaphor, the historical literature on state-building emphasizes that bureaucratic enclaves charged with delivering core state functions (e.g. territorial security, revenue generation) formed the building blocks of modern state formation (Tilly 1975; Brautigam et al. 2008). This was not necessarily in the sense that such PoEs offered rules-based routes towards Weberian forms of stateness, but rather that they were built on a politics of patronage that valued political loyalty as well as technocratic competence and that reflected the projects of particular rulers (Grindle 2012).

We set out to offer a more systematic account of what PoEs could reveal about the politics of state-building and development in contemporary Africa by applying the power domains framework to five countries with different types of political settlement.[4] This included two countries with relatively dominant settlements where power is more 'concentrated' around the governing coalition—Rwanda and Uganda—and three more competitive settlements where power is more 'dispersed'—Ghana, Kenya, and Zambia. These cases also offer variation within this continuum, with the configuration of power becoming less concentrated in Uganda and more concentrated in Zambia during the period under study here. Further variation is also apparent in terms of the social-foundations dimension of the political settlement, particularly in terms of how the ethno-regional calculus of coalition-building plays out and the potential for ruling elites to be subject to concerns with systemic vulnerability. This includes the contrast between cases where there

[4] This particular project was mainly funded by a separate grant from ESRC-DFID, with some additional funding from ESID, particularly for the Kenya case study undertaken by Matthew Tyce.

are clear minority–majority groupings (Rwanda) and more multi-ethnic settings, and where ethnic concerns were either predominant in such calculations (e.g. Kenya) or at least partly offset by political coalitions also forming around competing programmatic agendas (e.g. Ghana).

Researching PoEs

Researching PoEs presents several challenges, including the absence of subnational indices of government performance. To help identify high-performing bureaucratic agencies in each country we undertook expert surveys with public-sector professionals, politicians, donor officials, researchers, consultants, and representatives from both the private sector and civil society. Across the five cases, there was a general consensus that three different types of PoE could be identified: finance ministries (particularly budget departments), central banks, and revenue authorities. To offset problems of perception bias, we triangulated these survey results with data from a range of indexes to ensure that the criteria of being a PoE offered by Roll (2014) had been met—namely, a continued period of high performance over at least a five-year period in relation to the specific mandate of the organization and relative to other public-sector organizations in the same context. We generated performance indicators for each type of agency, including control of public spending for budget departments, the maintenance of both price and financial stability for central banks, and overall tax effort for revenue authorities (see Appendix II). We then conducted in-depth case studies of all fifteen organizations, examining the ups and downs of their performance since the early 1990s, before examining whether these performance patterns could be explained by political settlement dynamics, organizational-level factors (e.g. leadership), and other policy domain factors such as the organization's mandate and the policy function involved, as well as international support.

PoEs and State-building in Concentrated Political Settlements: The Contrasting Cases of Uganda and Rwanda

The trajectory of PoEs within the economic technocracies of Rwanda and Uganda reveals some instructive divergences. During the inclusive coalition-building phase of Uganda's political settlement under Museveni's dominant NRM, and amid soaring inflation in 1992, senior technocrats sold the idea of fiscal discipline to the President in the language of 'military' discipline. The president imposed a cash budget and granted the ministry of finance and central bank the heavyweight leadership and autonomy to deliver on their mandates. Heavily backed by multilateral and bilateral donors (Kuteesa et al. 2010), the Ministry of Finance, Planning, and Economic Development (MFPED) and the Bank of Uganda (BoU) delivered the fiscal discipline, macroeconomic stability, and social investments required to underpin a prolonged period of pro-poor economic growth (Bukenya and Hickey 2019). PoEs emerged here as a strategy of rule designed to maintain legitimacy among voters and international actors keen for countries in Africa to conform to the neoliberal model of development.

This deal started to unravel from the early 2000s, once power became more dispersed within Uganda's political settlement, including through increasingly competitive elections in 2001 and 2006. Senior officials within finance noted the ebbing-away of political support, with the president no longer persuaded that the technocratic route of economic stability and increased public expenditures via the budget process was delivering at the ballot box. A succession of weaker finance ministers was appointed, and officials also note the declining influence of donors during the mid-2000s, as Uganda graduated from debt and started to benefit from new flows of finance related to oil and Chinese investment. The Uganda Revenue Authority, which initially benefited from being granted semi-autonomous status in 1993, was undermined even earlier, with tax policy diluted and weak commissioner generals appointed from the 1997 elections (Kjær et al. 2017; Hickey 2023b).

The results of this retreat from supporting PoEs were striking: supplementary budgets exceeded their legal limits of 3 per cent of the overall budget every year from 2003 onwards, and Uganda's initially high PEFA rating declined between 2008 and 2012 (Bukenya and Hickey 2019). At the 2011 elections, both the MFPED and the BoU were effectively subject to political capture: supplementary budgets exceeded 25 per cent and—with the BoU reissuing old bank notes, which politicians used for vote-buying—inflation reached nearly 30 per cent (Golooba-Mutebi and Hickey 2016; Hickey and Matsiko 2023). Although the BoU moved swiftly to bring inflation back down, this loss of technocratic control helped generate a relative economic downturn, with economic growth averaging 4.4 per cent from 2012 to 2018 as compared to an average of over 7 per cent between 1992 and 2011. The Uganda Revenue Authority (URA), meanwhile, looked every inch a PoE from 2005 until 2014, as it benefited from the appointment of a highly competent and politically connected commissioner general and increased the tax contribution to the national budget from 58.7 per cent to 71.5 per cent between 2005 and 2014. However, the worsening tax-policy regime meant that tax-to-GDP ratio flatlined, and the overall rate of decline in tax effort apparent from

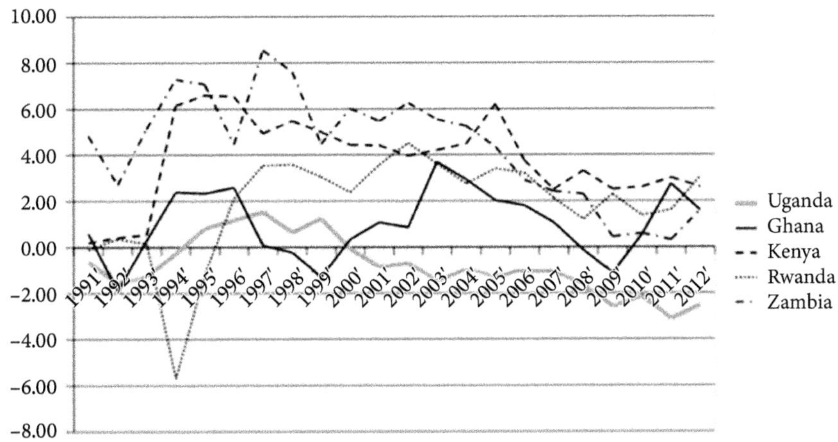

Figure 6.3 Tax effort in selected countries
Source: authors' calculations, from data in Youhou and Goujon (2017).

1997 was only temporarily slowed rather than reversed during this period (Figure 6.3).

The trajectory we identify in Rwanda was different in important respects, despite initial similarities with regards to the concentration of power within a revolutionary and militarized ruling coalition. After the genocide, the Ministry of Finance and Economic Planning (MINECOFIN) was so hollowed out that, when it resumed activity on 16 July 1994, only seven people reported to work (Chemouni 2019). However, and following a decade of political and international support, including allowing high-calibre ministers lengthy tenures, salary enhancements, and an effort to recruit the country's best graduates, the ministry had become, according to a World Bank study 'one of the more powerful finance ministries in the region' (World Bank 2013: 67), with an impressive profile of PEFA scores throughout the previous decade. The Banque Nationale Rwanda (BNR) also received strong support: its mandate for inflation control was enshrined in law in 2007, and the long-term tenures of three successive governors (only three from 2002 until 2020) offered further stability. Although droughts and commodity price fluctuations have led to price volatility in Rwanda, there is very little evidence of inflation arising from politicized hikes in public expenditure.

The Rwandan Revenue Authority has performed similarly well since gaining semi-autonomous status: the tax to GDP ratio increased markedly, from 10.8 per cent in 1998 to 16.7 per cent in 2017, and, in the second half of the 2010s, revenue increased by 10 per cent per year on average (Schreiber 2018: 10). Political leadership has been important, the president actively campaigning 'to change public attitudes towards paying taxes and corruption' (Fjeldstad and Moore 2009: 6). For one official, a habit of internal promotions 'means that you've got continuity and the culture of professionalism of the institution is preserved'.[5] Figure 6.3 reinforces the sense that Rwanda has performed well on tax effort in comparison to our other cases.

At first glance, the fact that the configuration of power has remained concentrated in Rwanda while becoming more dispersed in Uganda would seem to explain the different performance patterns we identify here. However, the patterns were actually different from the outset: whereas Uganda expended political capital only on building the capacity of a handful of agencies, Rwanda was engaged in a more generalized effort to develop high degrees of competence and autonomy across the public sector. This pattern, reflected in the World Governance Indicators (WGI) data in Figure 6.2, was confirmed by public-sector experts in Rwanda, who identify a pattern of state-building prioritization, with investments in capacity-building following the identification of specific policy priorities (Chemouni 2019).

This difference arguably flows from the social foundations of power in each case. In Rwanda, this has generated a sense of systemic vulnerability among the minority ruling elite owing to fears of a return to genocide that is best offset by building durable state institutions and delivering development (Doner et al. 2005; Slater 2010). In contrast, the absence of a systemic threat in Uganda has instead incentivized only minimal efforts to protect certain agencies amid a wider strategy of maintaining rule through a series of provisioning pacts.

PoEs and State-building in Dispersed Political Settlements: Offsetting the Pressures of Competitive Politics in Ghana, Kenya, and Zambia

Across all of our dispersed political settlements, we found that finance ministries, central banks, and revenue authorities have all struggled to maintain high levels of performance over prolonged periods. This has been particularly apparent in relation to the electoral cycle, although we also identify problems that flow from elite-level factionalism within ruling coalitions. Only for brief periods and under economically propitious conditions in the mid-2000s have technocratic coalitions between political leaders and senior bureaucrats managed to hold these pressures at bay.

[5] Interviewed in January 2019.

Ghana illustrates these general patterns well. As in Uganda, both the Ministry of Finance and the Bank of Ghana benefited during the 1980s from the political stability and reformist zeal offered by a dominant ruling coalition that had come to power after a prolonged period of political unrest. President Rawlings empowered trusted technocrats to run both institutions and benefited from direct capacity-building support from international actors keen for Ghana to implement structural adjustment reforms (Abdulai and Mohan 2019). Inflation was brought under control, and GDP grew at 6–7 per cent annually from 1984 to 1988, the highest in Africa at that time (Lyon 1997: 1).

However, the onset of competitive politics from the early 1990s saw the economic technocracy pressured to use the budget to dispense patronage (Hutchful 1997: 38). Excessive budgetary demands led the minister of finance to resign in 1995 and reduced the autonomy of the central bank (Figure 6.4). With further expenditure spikes at the 1996 elections, a political business cycle became established (Mosley and Chiripanhura 2016): the average budget deficit as a percentage of GDP at 9.5 per cent during election years as compared to 6.5 per cent for non-election years (Figure 6.5). The ministry also suffered from the large-scale turnover of staff that accompanied each election, with newly appointed ministers requested to work with civil servants 'they can trust'.[6]

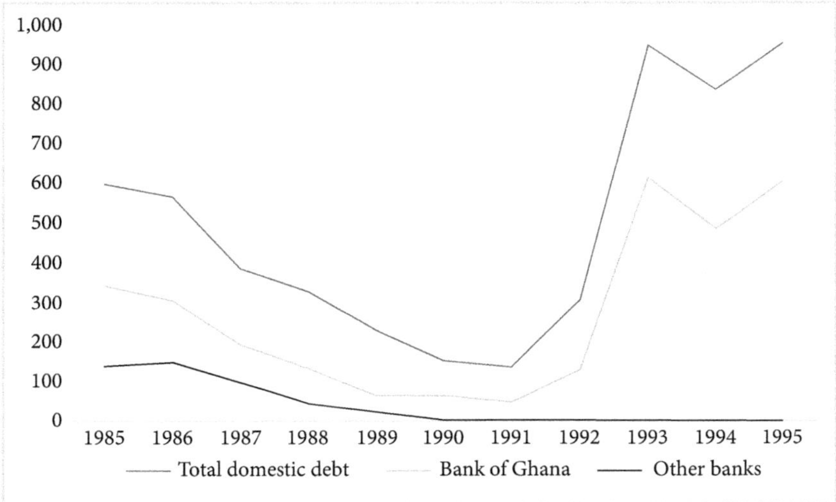

Figure 6.4 Central bank financing of the Government of Ghana, 1985–1995
Source: authors' calculations, based on World Bank data (1993: 29).

[6] Ministry of Finance divisional director, 16 May 2018.

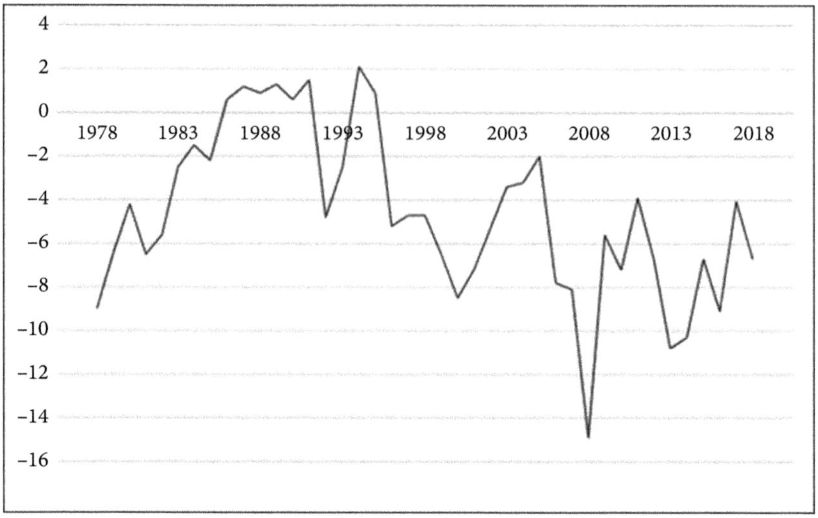

Figure 6.5 Budget deficits in Ghana (% of GDP), 1978–2018
Source: authors' calculations, based on data from Budget Unit, Ministry of Finance, Accra.

An exception was the surprising level of fiscal discipline during the 2004 election year. This derived from the trust that the new president placed in the ministerial leadership of Osafo Marfo, and his discipline in ensuring that expenditure increases in 2003 were below the rate of increases in tax collection and within budget ceilings (Republic of Ghana 2003). This in turn catalysed improvements in key macroeconomic indicators: the budget deficit was reduced from −8.5 per cent in 2000 to just −2 per cent by 2005, and inflation was reduced from over 40 per cent in 2000 to 11.8 per cent by 2005 (Debrah 2009: 103). Economic growth rates also increased from 3.7 per cent in 2000 to 5.9 per cent by 2005. The budget process was improved to the extent that Ghana became 'the regional leader on budget oversight and engagement in West Africa' (International Budget Partnership 2012: 3). However, Marfo was replaced immediately after the December 2004 elections, apparently because of 'the feeling within his party that he had denied them campaign funds'.[7]

PoEs in both Kenya and Zambia also experienced this phenomenon during the mid-2000s, with presidents building alliances with senior technocrats to protect the economic technocracy. In Kenya, the sense that the country possessed a strong and autonomous administration (Leys 1975; Opalo 2019) had unravelled during the 1980s under pressure from processes of elite fragmentation, state informalization, and externally driven reforms that

[7] Ministry of Finance divisional director, 16 May 2018; see Abdulai (2019).

further fragmented the state (Tyce 2020b). From 1992 until 2002, only the Central Bank of Kenya (CBK) delivered. Granted autonomy in 1993 and led by a new reformist governor, the CBK kept inflation rates within single figures for most of this period, save for a small blip during the 1997 election cycle. In contrast, the semi-autonomous status granted to the Kenya Revenue Authority (KRA) in 1995 had the opposite effect, as both tax revenues and tax effort declined between 1995 and 2002 (Figure 6.3). The KRA was undermined by the Treasury's inconsistent tax policies, including widespread tax exemptions deployed to secure elite allegiances (Southall 1999: 95). The Commissioner General had no legal security of tenure and ministerial board members 'intervened a lot' to shield particular businesses from scrutiny and to influence internal appointments.[8] The Treasury performed particularly poorly, with Kenya's economic growth rates and fiscal balance fluctuating significantly, often in tandem with election cycles.

After the 2002 election, however, President Kibaki built on his economic training and social network to appoint a series of loyal and highly competent leaders within the economic technocracy. The Treasury slashed debt levels and interest payments, kept deficits within agreed bounds, and contributed strongly to 'the only episode of five-year consecutive growth acceleration in the country's history' (Kimenyi et al. 2016: 2; Muchai and Muchai 2016). Although inflation rates increased during this period, this reflected a deliberate policy of undertaking large-scale productive investments and the CBK's pursuit of financial inclusion and private-sector credit (Dafe 2019). The biggest turnaround came with KRA, under a friend of the president, who became the first commissioner general to serve not only one full term but three.[9] With tax administration and policy pulling in similar directions, Kenya's tax-to-GDP and tax effort metrics improved strongly between 2003 and 2005 (Figure 6.3).

However, growing fragmentation within the ruling coalition from 2005 stalled this momentum. Restoring stability meant co-opting politicians through favourable tax policies, which ate into the KRA's potential revenues, while the president lost control of decision-making powers around key roles within the economic technocracy. After Kibaki left power in 2013, the negative impacts of inter-coalitional politics on PoE performance reached higher levels still. President Kenyatta had little ideational affinity with technocrats in the economic technocracy and both he and his Jubilee Coalition co-leader pressured the Treasury to accommodate their (uncoordinated) development

[8] Interview, ex-KRA official, Nairobi, 27 March 2019.
[9] Interview, PFM specialist, Nairobi, 12 April 2019.

projects.[10] Caught within a debilitating power struggle between the two coalition leaders, the KRA has been deployed as a political weapon for hounding enemies and a patronage tool for shielding allies, with revenue collections declining since 2014 (Tyce 2020c). Only the central bank performed well in the 2010s, delivering price stability and also increased financial stability under the strongly rules-based approach of a new governor.

In Zambia, the capacity of technocratic coalition to protect PoEs from difficult political settlement dynamics was similarly short-lived. Between 2003 and 2008, President Mwanawasa and Finance Minister Magande took advantage of favourable economic conditions, with Magande given the autonomy to operate and to invest in capacity-building within the ministry. He also drew on the president's anti-corruption reforms to impose a meritocratic approach to recruitment and appointments. Zambia's scores on PEFA indicators improved from 2005 to 2008, and, with the exception of a lapse at the 2006 elections, the previously high levels of fiscal indiscipline were reined in (Hinfelaar and Sichone 2019). During this period, GDP growth increased to 7.4 per cent per year on average and inflation was reduced from 22 per cent to 8 per cent. However, the death of Mwanawasa in 2008, and the subsequent death of another president in office in 2014, combined with highly competitive pressures to undermine this progress. Ruling coalitions became fluid and short-lived, with much shorter leadership postings to core agencies. PEFA indicators show a decline of budget discipline during this period, with a particular slump arriving with the attempts by President Lungu from 2015 onwards to impose a more concentrated form of political settlement. Whereas pre-2015 budgetary arrears were less than 2 per cent of total expenditure, this increased sharply to more than 10 per cent of total expenditure (PEFA 2017). The Zambia Revenue Authority (ZRA), which had benefited from credible leadership and capacity-building during the mid-2000s, became led by a crony of the president, who has been deployed to target the opposition (Hinfelaar and Cheelo 2021). After also experiencing a period of decline, the Bank of Zambia alone seems to be steadying, due largely to international pressures related to the country's growing debt crisis.

Discussion

Our findings strongly suggest that political settlements play a powerful role in shaping the uneven performance of PoEs over time in Africa. Other factors play a part—particularly organizational leadership and international

[10] Interview, PFM specialist, Nairobi, 12 April 2019.

support—but it is striking that many of our case-study organizations have had the same mandates, each of them critical to basic state functioning, and similar levels of international support over prolonged periods, and yet performance has fluctuated nonetheless. The distribution of political power plays a particularly important role, with dispersed patterns of power within ruling coalitions and between opposing factions generally limiting the autonomy and effectiveness of public-sector organizations. However, the social foundations of political settlements also matter. Only in one case, Rwanda, do we find evidence that this has generated the kind of systemic vulnerability that has encouraged political elites to build on and out from bureaucratic enclaves as part of a wider state-building strategy, as opposed to a more minimalist approach of governing via a handful of bureaucratic enclaves subject to the whims of presidential caprice (e.g. Uganda). This suggests that there are two different kinds of pathway through which PoEs might emerge in concentrated political settlements in relation to wider processes of state-building.

In contrast, our dispersed settlements all converged around a similar trajectory whereby technocratic coalitions of politicians and bureaucrats who shared similar ideas and often also identities were able to create a space within which PoEs could flourish. Importantly, in each of Ghana, Kenya, and Zambia this happened within the context of benign macroeconomic conditions during the mid-2000s, and in each case the period of high performance was also short-lived, often barely stretching to the definitive five-year timeframe suggested by Roll (2014). The social foundations of political settlements also seemed to have an effect in these dispersed cases, with the ethnicized politics of factionalism within Kenya's ruling coalitions particularly damaging to the performance of all but the most autonomous aspects of the economic technocracy. This contrasts somewhat with Ghana, where higher standards of government effectiveness have been achieved (Figure 6.2), perhaps because ethno-regional competition has been institutionalized within a loosely programmatic form of two-party politics.

Political settlement dynamics also directly shape organizational leadership, one of the other critical features of PoE performance. All of our high-performing cases involved leaders who were not just technically competent but also politically loyal and connected enough to be rewarded with the lengthy tenures required to build progressive organizational cultures and navigate difficult contexts. Whilst PoEs reflect certain aspects of Weberian stateness, as in their somewhat greater respect for meritocratic processes of recruitment and promotion, they also draw on (and can help sustain) the politics of patronage (Grindle 2012; Hickey 2019, 2023a).

The fact that our case-study organizations were all located within the economic technocracy is striking. This domain includes a number of organizations with legally enforced mandates that are often charged with delivering policy tasks of a logistical nature within relatively short governance chains (e.g. inflation targeting), in contrast to most aspects of social service delivery (Roll 2014). Moreover, the economic technocracy in Africa has arguably been subject to the highest levels of both international support and disciplinary power of any policy domain (Harrison 2010). This mixture of capacity-building and disciplinary oversight has had a profound effect, not only on these PoEs but also on the broader pattern of state-building and development in Africa. It arguably helped ensure the economic survival of several African countries, including in cases where inflation was out of control, and in turn the political survival of certain ruling coalitions. It has also empowered certain bureaucrats and offered them a degree of protection from political pressure. However, this has involved a highly partial approach to state capacity-building, one in which those parts of the state charged with delivering neoliberal reforms received support, whereas those associated with pursuing alternative development agendas were largely overlooked. The departments and ministries of trade, planning, commerce, and industry that had underpinned the developmental state miracles were conspicuously overlooked here, in ways that have foreclosed African states from developing the capacity to pursue the kinds of alternative, more productivist pathways that recent political economy trends may have otherwise enabled (Jepson 2020).

In strategic terms, then, an approach to improving governance and state-building via support for PoEs needs to be handled with caution. High-functioning enclaves can deliver important governance tasks that matter for maintaining economic and political stability, and that are largely logistical in nature. Such organizations benefit from leaders with political as well as technical skills and lengthy tenures, highly trained staff, positive organizational cultures, and exposure to international norms, expertise, and protection. All of these offer points for intervention. However, we found little evidence of PoEs playing an important role in delivering on the more difficult policy challenges involved in securing inclusive development (Pritchett and Woolcock 2004) and also some negative spillovers, whereby such organizations hoover up the best staff and can be misused to maintain ruling elites in power. It is also imperative that, if building high-performing government agencies are to be pursued by external actors, a much more balanced approach is required to choosing which parts of the state to support and in pursuit of which form of development. If ensuring structural transformation is the critical challenge for African countries today, our analysis strongly suggests the need to shift the focus towards building the capacity of a different set of state organizations in the future.

7
Conclusions and Implications

Our research echoes the now deafening insistence that politics plays a critical role in shaping developmental processes and outcomes, but goes further in offering systematic new insights into how this actually happens in practice. We find that the capacity and commitment to promote development are shaped primarily by the nature of the political settlement, in terms of the configuration of both political and social power therein, and the ways in which this shapes elite perceptions and incentives. Going further, we show that the specific ways in which this happens and the developmental outcomes that this leads to need to be understood in relation to particular policy domains. This 'power domains' analysis has offered greater traction in explaining contemporary development puzzles than current approaches, particularly those limited to a narrowly institutionalist approach. Questions that range from how countries can avoid the resource curse through to how governments can deliver higher-quality services to poor people all largely turn, we argue, on how the configuration of power shapes which institutions emerge and how they function, with coalitions acting as the mechanism through which these relationships are mediated.[1]

By examining certain *types* of power configurations, our approach enables us to go beyond the insistence that 'context matters', a statement that, while intrinsically true, is not helpful when it comes either to building theory or to generating strategic implications for wider usage.[2] Using a political settlements typology to guide comparative case-study analysis revealed two trajectories for successful developmental outcomes. The first involves a dominant ruling coalition with a strong developmental vision, which was

[1] Along with others, then, we see the notion of overlapping 'relational fields' or 'power domains' as being central to shifting the ontological focus to politics and power rather than institutions per se (e.g. Goldstone 2004); Sum and Jessop 201; Fligstein and McAdam 2015).

[2] In terms of theory, and as Portes (2006: 235) notes in his critique of the failure of neoinstitutionalism to specify the actual features of a social context that shape elite incentives, 'saying simply that everything depends on time and place leads us nowhere theoretically, as this statement is nonfalsifiable'. With regards to strategy, George and Bennett (2005: 7) argue that 'typological theories can guide researchers towards questions and research designs whose results will be pertinent to problems faced by policymakers. One of the chief goals of political science ... is to provide policymakers with "generic knowledge" that can help them form effective strategies.'

Pathways to Development. Sam Hickey and Kunal Sen, Oxford University Press.
 DOI: 10.1093/oso/9780198872566.003.0007

observed most clearly across multiple domains in both Ethiopia (e.g. social assistance) and Rwanda (e.g. maternal health, gender equity). Where dominance is joined by a configuration of social power that presents an existential threat to the ruling coalition, this can result in more widespread commitment to institution-building and development; where this is absent, then the commitment and capacity to deliver are limited to specific domains and are vulnerable to the caprice of unaccountable leaders, as in the experience of Pockets of Effectiveness (PoEs) in Uganda's oil and economic policy domains and of education in Cambodia. The second trajectory involves competitive settlements within which the problematic tendencies emanating from this kind of context, including the generally short-term vision of ruling elites and the politicization of the public bureaucracy, are offset by the presence of strong and coherent coalitions within particular policy domains. Often limited to short periods of time, some national-level examples here include the roles of PoEs in the economic policy domains of countries such as Ghana, Kenya, and Zambia, of economic growth and some social provisioning in Bangladesh, education in Ghana, and the slow but steady promotion of social assistance in more competitive settings, particularly Kenya and Zambia. This is also apparent at the more local level, whereby the uneven provision of high-quality social provisioning in Ghana and Uganda is explicable in terms of whether or not developmental coalitions had been formed at local levels between key actors, including politicians, bureaucrats, traditional leaders and citizens. These coalitions offer an interesting variant of the civil–political society linkages emphasized as being critical to how states deliver human development, and not simply economic growth (Heller and Evans 2010; Heller 2013). This also reinforces the sense that the nature of the policy domain matters here, with different types of political settlement dealing better with some types of policy challenge than others, an issue to which we return below.

The social configuration of power and the power of ideas within political settlements also emerged as significant here. We found that the strength of response from ruling elites to specific development problems was shaped both by the level of perceived threat posed by social groups and by the relative significance of the groups to whom they felt the need to respond. This was particularly apparent in the case of social assistance, whereby the extent to which ruling elites perceived there to be a threat to the political settlement and their political survival within this closely predicted their level of response. Although donor-driven efforts to form policy coalitions around this new policy agenda were central to gaining traction within the policy domain, it was only once the perceived benefits of social assistance became aligned with the dominant ideas and interests within specific political settlements that any commitment to national-level roll-outs emerged. Importantly, the form that this response took was closely shaped by elite ideas, with both Ethiopia and Rwanda limiting their commitment to the cash transfer 'handouts' preferred by donors, and placing a much stronger emphasis on public works programmes. In the case of elites passing legislation to protect women from domestic violence, women's movements had to frame their claims carefully within prevailing norms to avoid antagonizing veto players. Paradigmatic ideas that bind elites together, such as around the importance of education to nation-building and modernity, can help offset the damaging consequences of inter-elite factionalism, as we arguably see within the education domain in Bangladesh and Ghana. Such ideas, and the policies that flow from them, can be particularly difficult to challenge in dominant political settlements, as in the cases of Rwanda's rapid shift in the language of instruction and the refusal of the president of Uganda to reconsider the populist promise of 'free education', despite the apparent need for more creative solutions to the problem of financing education.

As such, we would argue that ideas are foundational to both the formation and the functioning of political settlements, whereby certain paradigmatic ideas help to bind elites to certain institutional arrangements, and political agency is shown to be shaped by normative ideas as well as material interests. Although not devoid of instrumental interests—the RPF in Rwanda is driven by fear of a return to genocide as well as ideological commitment to development—this emphasis ensures a focus on the 'role' as well as the 'structure' that states need to adopt to be considered developmental (Vu 2007). This focus on ideas runs through our power domains framework. Ideas are critical at the level of the policy domain too: in the process of framing certain problems as in need of solutions, and of the nature these solutions should take. Finally, ideas also matter in the local realm of power relations, where elite projects of state-building and development actually hit the ground. Such processes often involve everyday clashes between different ideas around issues of political legitimacy, agency, rights, and who deserves to get what from processes of resource allocation. Ideas are not separate from but form the very stuff of politics.

As hinted at above, the character of the policy domain is also critical, particularly in terms of the role it plays in maintaining the political settlement and the type of policy challenge involved. Instructive here is the sense that different types of settlement may generate different types of state capacity, which in turn enables them to make progress on certain types of policy challenges, but not others. For example, the evidence that Rwanda has been slow to improve learning outcomes for primary-school children, as compared to greater progress in more competitive settlements that exhibit much higher levels of dysfunctionality within their public sectors, may suggest that dominant settlements are less able to deliver on transactional policy challenges as compared to more logistical ones (Andrews et al. 2012). Whereas logistical challenges are amenable to being met through strong, top-down forms of accountability and performance management, transactional challenges such as learning require multiple forms of accountability and information flows that seem likelier to emerge in the more open political spaces offered within competitive settings. This also has implications for governance arrangements, with PoEs generally far more capable of dealing with logistical rather than transactional policy challenges.

Another important finding here is that countries may arrive at fairly similar developmental outcomes through very different pathways. This sense of equifinality is most evident in the case of progress on maternal mortality outcomes, whereby dominant Rwanda and competitive Bangladesh achieved similar outcomes, but through very different routes. As such, a typology of political settlements might prove less useful for performing comparisons across type in relation to development outcomes per se, than in helping to reveal the particular pathways that are open to achieving development progress within given types of political settlement. This finding that political settlements offer distinct pathways through which development can be achieved in particular policy domains is highly relevant for current efforts to ensure that development interventions achieve a clear 'fit' with particular types of context.

What Does This Mean for Rethinking the Politics of Development?

The new turn to politics within international development has helped ensure that the long-standing focus on 'institutions' has been joined by a deeper understanding of the ways in which politics and power relations shape which institutions emerge and how they function in practice. This has been particularly important in reordering the causal chain of inference, whereby the configuration of power takes ontological precedence over institutions, and coalitions act as the mechanism through which these relationships are mediated. However, this raises several questions with regards to the gap between long-range theories of historical change and pressing contemporary concerns around development progress.

Our approach here has been to extend the intellectual reach of the current political turn into the realm of particular 'policy domains' within which struggles of development ideas and resources take place. Having road-tested the resulting 'power domains' approach through systematic comparative case-study analysis of key development puzzles, our sense is that this approach offers a significant contribution to fulfilling what Merilee Grindle has identified as the 'missing middle' in the new politics and development agenda, at the level of both theory and, as discussed below, strategy. Theoretically, a power domains approach is most useful for explaining how development unfolds over more proximate timeframes than is possible within the *longue durée* addressed within historical institutionalism. With others (Centeno et al. 2017), we are mainly concerned with the contemporaneous social and political forces that shape the deployment of state capacity and the emergence of elite commitment to development, and that can help us to understand the variations that emerge among otherwise similar types of state in terms of their development progress.[3] From this perspective, our focus on political settlements, which are dynamic and shaped by agents such as leaders and coalitions as well as structural factors (Leftwich and Wheeler 2011), offers a means of understanding and explaining what happens *within* periods of relative equilibrium, as defined in terms of particular types of political settlement. What our analysis draws attention to is the extent to which significant shifts in orientation and progress towards development can occur within such periods, in ways that can profoundly shape a country's trajectory and the well-being of its citizens. This strongly suggests that, whereas historical institutionalist accounts may be able to identify the structural capacities with which a given state is endowed, this needs to be joined by a close reading of how the contemporary configuration of power shapes whether these capacities are actually deployed in ways that enable states actually to perform.

The inclusion of policy domains in our framework further enables us to bridge the macro–micro divide in current governance thinking and reflect the evidence that politics played out differently within different types of field or sector. Here we conceive of policy domains, not as a separate or wholly distinct space or sphere, but rather as a field of power relations that overlaps with other such fields (Goldstone 2004), the most immediate and powerful one

[3] There are links here also to the mode of analysis pursued by Merilee Grindle in her (2012) study of patronage in the public service, where she integrates historical institutionalism with an analysis of the role played by reformers and coalitions at particular moments in time (although political settlements analysis might be better situated as attempting to fill the 'missing middle' between these two perspectives).

being the political settlement. The role that policy domains play in terms of generating rents and/or legitimacy for ruling coalitions is particularly critical: this shapes the extent to which such domains are characterized by embedded autonomy or some form of capture, and has a significant influence over the ways in which they function and their developmental character. Policy domains can sometimes, in return, have powerful effects on political settlements. This occurs particularly where they are thick with rents and central to the country's political economy (as with natural resources—see Bebbington et al. 2018), but also, albeit to a lesser extent, where they are capable of catalysing bottom-up pressures (as with cash transfers). Finally, our work on education, health, and also the implementation of gender-equity policies emphasizes the importance of extending a power-domains perspective to the local level, where much of the real action around developmental progress takes place.

Context, Coalitions, and Capacity: The Strategic Implications of Taking Politics Seriously

Three main strategic implications can be identified as flowing from the power domains perspective applied in this volume—namely, the importance of context, capacity, and coalitions. *Context*, we already knew, is critical in shaping development outcomes. This awareness has already helped steer development policy away from the universalizing and ideological tendencies of promoting best-practice institutions irrespective of locational differences. What we and others (e.g. Levy 2014) are arguing is that context matters in particular and identifiable ways, predominantly through the ways in which specific types of political settlement shape how institutions actually function in practice. Our identification of the different pathways to development success that emerge within different types of political settlement gives greater definition to calls for 'best-fit' approaches (Andrews et al. 2017), encouraging efforts to ensure that policy-reform efforts are attuned to the incentives and ideas that flow from these different political conditions. However, and while this support calls for thinking and working politically to be at the heart of development cooperation, it does not necessarily point towards reforms that 'go with the grain' and risk reinforcing certain regressive tendencies within given political settlements. Our research into how new and potentially transformative policy agendas come to gain traction suggests that bending too far towards the grain can result in reforms either being diluted and distorted, as in certain examples of anti-domestic violence legislation (Ahikire and

Mwiine 2019), or reinforcing personalized rather than more developmental forms of patronage, as with cash transfers (Hickey and Bukenya 2019b).

Coalitions emerge as critical mechanisms through which the often messy dynamics of political settlements are successfully navigated in pursuit of more progressive development outcomes. Three different types of coalitions emerged as being particularly critical here: ruling coalitions that occupy the apex of political settlements; agenda-setting policy coalitions that operate in relation to specific domains; and delivery coalitions that are involved in the often local-level implementation of specific interventions. Policy coalitions form a particularly important locus of intervention. In policy domains that are central to the survival or legitimacy of the ruling coalition, we found that ruling elites form strong policy coalitions with bureaucratic actors and often donors in order to achieve politically significant reforms and goals. This includes pacts between political elites, leading bureaucrats, and international agencies around economic growth and macroeconomic stability, natural-resource governance, and (sometimes) public-sector reform. An outcome of these coalitions is often bureaucratic 'pockets of effectiveness', which we return to below in relation to state capacity. Such coalitions can provide powerful protection for specific policy agendas and may block new ones emerging, as we found in the cases of neoliberal economic-policy reform and also the emphasis on access to education rather than educational quality. The policy takeaway here is that the first step to achieving reforms might not be to devise a new policy agenda per se but rather to undertake the somewhat messier work of building coalitions that can bring together the interests, ideas, and actors required to navigate opposing interests and ideas, formulate new policies, and ensure that they gain traction. External actors and ideas can play important roles, as with cash transfers and anti-domestic violence legislation, although it is the agency of reformist bureaucrats, politicians, and civil-society movements that is most important here.

Delivery coalitions can play a critical role at subnational levels, particularly around the delivery of high-quality health and education. In the absence of settlement-level pressures for high performance throughout a given policy domain, local-level coalitions of political, bureaucratic, and social actors emerge as the main route through which institutional fixes are devised and implemented. Examples include the district-level delivery of health services in Uganda and of education in Ghana, with developmental coalitions emerging as central to either driving through national reforms or finding ways around the problems created by political (dis)incentives, policy incoherence, and unsuitable governance arrangements, and achieving much better results than directly comparable districts.[4] The nature of patron–client relations means that these coalitions are not separate from the workings of the national political settlement: in Uganda, the leading players in both our high- and low-performing districts around health were all members of the ruling coalition; in Ghana, the same competitive pressures that shape sectoral performance at the national level were also apparent at the district level, with the low-performing district subject to more intense inter-party competition than our higher-performing district. The role of coalitions at multiple levels opens up new if far from straightforward opportunities for donors to engage productively with the politics of development. Growing awareness of how such coalitions can be supported (DLP 2012; Booth and Unsworth 2014) can now be applied to new frontiers, including the need for stronger policy coalitions around higher-quality education and industrial policy.

State *capacity*, our third and final 'c', emerges as critical across the full range of policy domains surveyed here. The state remains the only institution capable of protecting national interests against the predations of transnational capital (as around natural-resource governance), delivering rapid economic growth while providing Polanyian protection from commodification, protecting women from patriarchy, and delivering public goods on a wide scale. Within policy domains charged with delivering largely logistical policy challenges, state capacity may be most effectively built and deployed in the form of bureaucratic 'pockets of effectiveness' (Roll 2014). Such PoEs proved capable of securing the kinds of 'deals environment' required to protect the national interest around natural-resource governance, accelerate economic growth (Chapter 3), and underpin fiscal discipline, macroeconomic stability, and revenue generation (Chapter 6). This suggests that PoEs should form part of a more realistic governance agenda than has hitherto characterized public-sector reform agendas, although their apparent absence from policy domains characterized more by transactional policy challenges reveals the limits of this approach. We also found strong grounds to challenge the ideological bias towards neoliberal forms of state-building that has left African states ill-equipped to move beyond the basics of macroeconomic management and with few of the capabilities required to address more challenging policy agendas, such as achieving structural transformation. Future efforts to support PoEs need to be more balanced in nature and tilted towards the developmental trajectories prioritized by national governments themselves.

[4] In other ESID research not reported on here we found that in competitive clientelist settings such as India's, where 'state transformation is complex, messy, contested, unpredictable and generally unplanned' (Burra et al. 2016: 41), civil-society engagement has been significant in delivering pro-poor housing in Indian cities, through a co-production of solutions with local bureaucrats and engineers.

By highlighting the importance of state capacity, there is a risk of broadening the apparent divide between those proposing a 'realist' as opposed to a more 'normative' agenda for governance and development in the global south. Here, one school of thinking on the politics of long-run development emphasizes 'openness' and 'inclusion' (Acemoglu and Robinson 2012), while the other focuses on 'capacity' (e.g. Fukuyama 2013, 2016). We would certainly argue for a stronger focus on state capacity than has hitherto been the case and for greater recognition that it is immensely challenging for polities to manage two major processes of political development—namely, competitive politics and state-building—at the same time. The difficulties of governing multi-party politics in weak institutional contexts is well understood within historical studies of state formation and patronage (Grindle 2012) and suggests that greater attention is required to issues of how reforms can be sequenced, as indicated in the 'good-enough governance' agenda (Grindle 2004). However, we would make two further points here. The first is that an emphasis on state capacity need not be associated with a conservative return to 'order'; rather, a historical reading of the literature on how social democracy emerged in the global south as well as the global north clearly indicates that state formation needs to reach a certain level before conditions are amenable for more progressive political formations to emerge (Sandbrook et al. 2007). Second, there now appears to be a growing acceptance of the need not only to consider questions of both state capacity and inclusion and accountability together, but also of the importance of coalitions as the mechanism through which this process can occur: as Acemoglu and Robinson (2019: 31) note in *The Narrow Corridor*: 'New coalitions are critical for the state to gain greater capacity while keeping its shackles.'

Final Thoughts

> How growth, democracy and redistribution—all profoundly disruptive and transformative processes—are integrated and reconciled is perhaps the greatest challenge of all. It is essentially a political challenge to be resolved politically, not through one-size-fits-all economic models. It is, after all, the problem of how to create social democracy in the tropics.
>
> **(Leftwich 2005: 596)**

In emphasizing that there are different pathways towards social justice, all of which are closely shaped by politics and power relations, there is a risk of adding further fuel to ongoing debates on the relationship between democracy and development (van de Walle 2016). Of all the new variants of political theorizing within the new turn to politics, political settlements analysis has provoked the most controversy, particularly regarding its proposition that a degree of dominance may offer greater developmental benefits than intense political competition. Such findings and debates are not new. Feminists have long noted that democratic transitions have often failed to help secure recognition of women's rights (Waylen 2007), comparative political scientists accept that social provisioning is as closely informed by patron–client politics as by formal democracy (Carbone 2009), and early work on developmental states was clear that the absence of democracy was arguably an enabling factor (Leftwich 1995). Nor do our findings all point in the same direction. We have also shown how democratic pressures, albeit fed through the logic of patron-client relationships, have been significant in driving up levels of social assistance in Kenya and Zambia, and helped secure higher levels of oversight and accountability around social provisioning than in more dominant settings. There is also a broader sense that the 'inclusive' forms of 'competitive clientelism' that we witness in Ghana and Bangladesh, as opposed to the more exclusive (or predatory) forms apparent in countries such as Guinea-Bissau and perhaps Nigeria, may over the longer run be building state institutions with the capacity to deliver (see Grzymala-Busse 2008), particularly where clientelism takes place around well-institutionalized political organizations with at least some programmatic agendas, as in Ghana (Hickey 2023a). This is less likely to occur as rapidly as through the more impartial and arguably stronger institutions that some dominant party settlements seem able to develop, but still compares favourably to the more personalized and less institutionalized forms of vote-buying witnessed in 'weak dominant' settings, such as Uganda.

From an analytical perspective, these apparent problems around the democracy-development debate are relatively easy to resolve. Given the absence of clarity from the macro-data on the links between democracy and development, and as Tim Kelsall's seminal review (2014) points out, these questions are best approached in the way we have tried to do here: through analysing not the formal trappings of democracy but of the actual workings of power and political settlements in particular (and comparable) contexts. The normative question is arguably more difficult to settle and is not entirely distinct: our theoretical choices are also normative ones, in that they draw attention to the aspects of the world that we (a priori) judge to be important. While we share the central focus of political settlements analysis on questions of power and relations of power in particular, this leaves open a great deal of room for manoeuvre as to how power is conceptualized and which forms of power relations fall under the microscope. This book has started to articulate how different ontological starting points, particularly around notions of power, can take the current turn to political explanations for development in different directions, including how particular forms of agency (most notably in the form of coalitions) can achieve significant shifts, despite apparently binding structural constraints.

This critical focus on relations of power may help enable a clearer conversation between political settlements analysis and wider issues of social justice. Questions of social justice do not ultimately rest on questions of redistribution and recognition alone; rather, the uneven distribution of rights and resources that undermines prospects for inclusive development inheres in unequal relationships of power (e.g. Fraser 2008). In drawing closer attention to the role that power relations play, the power domains framework employed here has started to offer a clearer sense of how the politics of development actually plays out in practice, and of the kinds of agency and ideas required to shift this in more progressive directions. If there is a case for going further in weaving together realist forms of political analysis with a more normative sense of the politics of social justice, the turn towards a relational perspective that is increasingly evident across the social sciences would seem to offer the clearest intellectual route forward for such a project.[5]

[5] See Hickey (2023a) and forthcoming work by Clare Cummings for an effort to combine political-settlements analysis with critical political theory. Going beyond the work on 'relational fields' already referenced here (Goldstone 2004; Fligstein and McAdam 2015), this relational approach to social justice has its origins in feminist and post-Marxist thinking (see Hickey 2014) and might be seen as the more radical edge of what is now becoming a broader turn to placing relations at the centre of social science theorizing (Jessop 2007; Dépelteau 2013).

APPENDICES

APPENDIX I

Key Country Contexts

This appendix gives thumbnail sketches of the main countries where we undertook original research into the politics of development, with a cut-off date of 2020. We divide these between two main types of political settlement, differentiated in terms of the configuration of power within each—namely, 'competitive' scenarios where ruling coalitions are subject to relatively high levels of inter-elite competition for power (Bangladesh, Ghana, India, Kenya, and Zambia), and, conversely, settlements where ruling coalitions are more 'dominant' (Cambodia, Ethiopia, Rwanda, South Africa, and Uganda). We also briefly discuss the social configuration of power within each case.

Competitive Political Settlements

Bangladesh

Through the 1970s and 1980s, Bangladesh was characterized by dominant party rule, initially under the Awami League until 1975, and then under military–authoritarian leaderships.[1] The return to parliamentary democracy in 1991 ushered in a period of competitive clientelism. Through the 1990s and the 2000s, power alternated between the country's two main political parties, the Bangladesh Nationalist Party (BNP) and Awami League (AL), except for a brief period in 2007–9, when a caretaker government under the aegis of the military was in place. A feature of this settlement that differentiates it importantly from other competitive–clientelist settlements—for example, Ghana—is that there has been a lack of credible third-party enforcement of electoral rules to ensure that incumbent governments are not using administrative power to affect election outcomes (Khan 2013: 65). Consequently, the threat of political violence has not diminished over time, and there has been little progression towards more impersonal institutions. However, other changes are afoot: there have been strong signs that Bangladesh's political settlement is shifting towards dominance, most notably since 2014, when the BNP boycotted national elections, underlining the decline in party political competition and a growing sense that power is being consolidated under the ruling AL. However, most of our research on Bangladesh relates to the period when competitive clientelism clearly prevailed (between 1991 and 2013), and thus for the purposes of this study the country falls in the competitive category.

Under competitive clientelism, the BNP and AL have been incentivized to operate in pursuit of short-term gains, maximizing the extraction of rents and distribution of benefits to the ruling coalition. This has led to significant politicization of the bureaucracy, evidenced by the systematic demotion and promotion of public servants during each party's rule. The influence of the ruling party of the day, and the importance of allegiance, is felt across society, through the business sector, media, and wider civil society. A further effect has been the prioritization of policies that have electoral traction, and the neglect of those that do not. For example,

[1] For a more detailed discussion of the political settlement in Bangladesh, see Hassan (2013) and Khan (2013).

reforms orientated towards improving gender relations and the condition of women, such as on domestic violence (DV) legislation, have to some extent been neglected or poorly implemented, because they bring neither electoral advantage nor scope for distributing patronage (Nazneen 2019). It is true that the important historical role that women have played within key moments of political settlement formation in Bangladesh—including their brutal treatment during the war with Pakistan—has enabled them to claim important political and social entitlements, including a quota for representation in parliament and large-scale social transfer programmes. Nevertheless, the approach of ruling elites to women remains largely paternalist. Indeed, this is also apparent in the general treatment of lower-class groups (Hossain 2017). There is little evidence that the social configuration of power in Bangladesh, an ethnically homogenous society within which caste-based hierarchies remain important, generates any significant threat perceptions among the ruling elite.

Despite unpropitious dynamics generated by competitive clientelism, Bangladesh has experienced impressive economic growth and poverty reduction. This arguably stems from an ability to reach ordered deals among the elite (Hassan and Raihan 2017) (particularly in the ready-made garments sector), and to some degree also an elite consensus about supporting the poor and avoiding the humanitarian crises seen in the 1970s (Hossain 2017).

Ghana

Since the return to multi-party democracy in 1992, Ghana too has represented a case of a competitive–clientelist political settlement, characterized by competition between the two main political forces, the National Democratic Congress (NDC) and the New Patriotic Party (NPP).[2] Power alternated in 2000, 2008, and 2016, with elections usually swung by very small margins. As such, excluded elite factions have always been a powerful force that ruling coalitions have had to contend with. The fact that each party has needed considerable mobilizing power at local levels to win closely fought elections has also deepened the power of local-level factions within each party. Other local actors, such as traditional authorities, frequently wield considerable influence over issues of natural-resource governance (Abdulai 2017; Frederiksen 2017). While the ideological roots of the main parties differ—with the NDC identifying more as social democratic and statist, and the NPP as pro-market—in practice, the awareness of the likelihood of losing power in the near future has a more significant bearing on the behaviour of successive governments than programmatic commitments. This pressure orientates governments towards short-term gains (rather than more sustainable transformations whose fruits might become apparent only some while after the current electoral cycle), including rent extraction to accumulate resources, recouping losses incurred through elections, and distributing resources according to the logics of political patronage (Oduro et al. 2014; Whitfield et al. 2015). With competition between some of the country's main ethno-territorial cleavages largely institutionalized within political party competition, the main threats to ruling elites are generated by rival elite factions and also the lower-level factions—or party 'footsoldiers'—on whom they rely for mobilizing political support and whose demands on public-sector resources (e.g. jobs) are difficult to overlook.

The pressures and incentives brought through the system of competitive clientelism are felt widely across Ghana's public and private sectors and can help explain many of the developmental outcomes observed. Successive governments face little incentive significantly to improve the efficiency of the public sector, which has meant that public-sector reform has

[2] For a more detailed discussion of the political settlement in Ghana, see Oduro et al. (2014).

had little impact (Appiah and Abdulai 2017). Key state appointments are under direct political control, which offers few incentives for bureaucrats to act against the interests of the ruling party and has helped further politicize the public administration. Newly elected governments typically remove public servants who are perceived as being aligned to the opposition in favour of appointing party loyalists.

India

Following independence from Britain in 1947 and the founding of the new republic in 1950, India's parliamentary democracy was dominated by the Indian National Congress—the main party force behind independence and a broadly centre-left party—until the mid-1970s.[3] Since then the political scene has been vigorously competitive at both state and national levels. The Congress and the right-leaning and Hindu nationalist Bharatiya Janata Party (BJP) are the main two parties nationally, but there is also a common practice of party alliances and coalitions for electoral purposes, spurred by a fractionalization of politics amid the rise of many smaller and regional parties (Sen et al. 2014: 26).

Compared to most other countries in our study, India is closer to what can be called a 'competitive–institutionalized' settlement (as opposed to competitive–clientelist), in that state activity has in some respects moved away from personalized relations to more Weberian, rule-based, impersonal functioning. This is particularly so in the judiciary and the office of the Controller and Auditor General. However, rent-sharing arrangements between politicians and businesses are still a feature of Indian politics, as are informal payments for preferred positions within the bureaucracy, and a good deal of petty low-level corruption. As such, it is probably more accurate to say that India represents a hybrid case in terms of the degree of formal institutionalization (Mehta and Walton 2014: 10).

A further important shift in the political settlement can be understood as taking place in its ideational element. The 'cognitive maps' typically held among elites have undergone a general shift from a state-led paradigm of economic development, rather wary of the market, following independence, to a more pro-market set of norms starting in the 1980s and accelerating in the 1990s, as elites came to believe that Indian industry could compete internationally and that deregulation would spur growth (Mehta and Walton 2014). This, in combination with the nature of relationships between political and economic elites, has contributed to episodic growth and deceleration. Between 1993 and 2002 a set of informal but relatively predictable and open relationships ('ordered deals') between political and economic elites saw a period of high growth. Between 2002 and 2011, these 'deals' became more closed, leading to negative feedback effects from accountability institutions, the middle class, and non-elites, along with structural retrogression of the economy. The years immediately after 2011 saw a growth deceleration and increasingly disordered deals (Sen et al. 2014).

Kenya

A competitive–clientelist political settlement emerged in Kenya in the early 1990s, disrupting the political dominance of the Kenya African National Union (KANU).[4] Initially, this offered opportunities to lower-level factions which became instrumental in mobilizing voters, yet

[3] For a more detailed discussion of the political settlement in India, see Mehta and Walton (2014).

[4] For a more detailed discussion of the political settlement in Kenya, see Wanyama and McCord (2017: 6–9) and Tyce (2020b: 5–9).

KANU remained in power under the leadership of President Moi. The 1990s were characterized by pervasive rent-seeking, with economic resources diverted to maintain KANU leaders and wider patronage networks. The election of the National Rainbow Coalition (NARC) in 2002 brought a broad alliance into power, incorporating a number of minor parties, on the basis of a commitment to addressing regional and political exclusion. President Kibaki's two terms in power (2002–13) oversaw strong economic growth on the basis of national development plans, protections offered to key economic institutions, an increasing role for civil society, and a range of new social protection measures. However, patronage and rent-seeking continued and returned to the fore when Kibaki's coalition fragmented from 2005. The Kibaki–NARC period of rule was even more profoundly interrupted in 2008 by the eruption of post-election violence. Ethno-territorial loyalties have long informed the political configuration of power in Kenya, and the largest groups, the Kikuyus and Luos, have had to form alliances with either each other or smaller groups such as the Kalenjin, Luhya, and Maasai to form ruling coalitions. Unlike in Ghana, where constitutional rules concerning political party formation largely warded off the possibility, in Kenya political organization and mobilization have a strongly ethno-territorial basis, both within and between parties. The use of state patronage to balance the claims of competing factions and lineages has generally kept Kenya stable, albeit at the cost of the high levels of corruption associated with such 'provisioning' pacts. However, in 2008 that balancing act failed, with the contested 2007 election results giving way to high levels of politically motivated interethnic violence. The damaging effects of this conflict on interethnic relations and state–society relations more broadly led to a period of constitutional reform and efforts by leaders to restore a contract of sorts between rulers and ruled.

Nonetheless, Kibaki's coalitions became increasingly fractured during his rule, culminating in the election of President Uhuru Kenyatta and the Jubilee Party of Kenya in 2013. Kenyatta discontinued the effort to protect key economic policies and ministries from rent-seeking, and, following the highly contentious 2017 elections in particular, his fractious coalition with Vice-President Ruto reduced the coherence of policymaking and ensured that public-sector governance has been fully exposed to ethnically informed intra-elite factionalism.

Zambia

Zambia's political settlement can be characterized as having been competitive–clientelist since the 1991 defeat of the long-ruling socialist United National Independence Party (UNIP) by the more centrist Movement for Multi-Party Democracy (MMD).[5] Power has alternated several times between these two parties and a party formed by a breakaway from the MMD, the left-populist Patriotic Front (PF). Another MMD-breakaway party, the liberal United Party for National Development (UPND), has also become a significant opposition party.

Perhaps the key aspect of Zambia's post-colonial settlement is the prevalence of a coalitional style of politics necessitated by a societal context featuring different ethnolinguistic groupings made salient under colonial rule: Bemba (43 per cent of the population), Nyanja (18 per cent), Tonga (including Ila and Lenje, 19 per cent), Lozi (8 per cent), and the north-west region (12 per cent) (Scarritt 2006). As these figures suggest, none of the groupings is large enough to dominate alone. Electoral politics has generally involved attempts to form ruling coalitions with broad buy-in across these groups, with elites receiving rent-seeking opportunities, and followers integrated through patronage networks. In the 1990s (continuing dynamics already observable under UNIP pre-1991), the need to maintain such coalitions led

[5] For a more detailed discussion of the political settlement in Zambia, see Pruce and Hickey (2019).

to a significant increase in ministerial positions awarded to elites, with an attempt to shore up horizontally inclusive coalitions through balancing these positions across representatives of different groupings. While social protection measures such as agricultural and food subsidies have also served as tools for the government to foster political support, in practice, maintaining elite privileges has often been prioritized over development. During economic downturns, for example, social services have tended to suffer, while benefits to elites within the ruling coalition have been maintained. This reflects the combination of the group-based social foundations of power with the clientelist nature of politics in Zambia. The emphasis on building horizontally inclusive coalitions (inclusive of elite representatives of the various ethnolinguistic groups) has generated stability in Zambia, but has come at the cost of high levels of clientelist patronage and an emphasis on inter-elite bargaining that seldom includes prolonged consideration of the developmental needs or rights of citizens (Lindemann 2011).

The arrival of the MMD, along with economic liberalization, disrupted the traditional loyalties between elites and lower-level factions, resulting in more dynamic ruling coalitions. Political divides have emerged on new fronts. In both 1991, with the victory of the MMD, and in 2011, with the Patriotic Front (PF), urban areas have provided crucial support. More recently, political parties have become increasingly personalized and detached from any coherent programmatic mandate. Since 2015, there have been clear signs that the PF's President Lungu is seeking to shift Zambia towards a more dominant form of settlement, with repeated efforts to close down political space for both opposition parties and civil society.

Dominant Political Settlements

We now turn to cases where ruling coalitions are more dominant, albeit to differing degrees.

Cambodia

After violent disorder in much of the mid-twentieth century, the disastrous regime of the Khmer Rouge from 1975 to 1978, and Vietnamese occupation from 1978 to 1992, stability emerged following the coup d'état led by now-Prime Minister Hun Sen in 1997.[6] Since 1998, Cambodia's political settlement has been based on the dominance of the Cambodian People's Party (CPP), under the leadership of Hun Sen, and in coalition with a wider set of actors, including business tycoons, the military, foreign investors, and international donors. The CPP maintains dominance through the delicate management of powerful factions, with the party, military, and business elites receiving significant opportunities for rent-seeking and offering patronage to followers. High-profile sackings of senior leaders are rare. The general population, meanwhile, is largely appeased by the strong economic growth that this settlement has enabled, and by popular social provisioning, in which donors have played significant roles. Political dominance is also maintained through a legitimating ideology rooted in a long history of political conflict, particularly the final defeat of the Khmer Rouge in the late 1990s. Although initially a Marxist-Leninist party in the mid-twentieth century, from around 1991 the CPP has morphed into a conservative and pro-market party.

Although the CPP has won three successive elections, it has also faced growing challenges to its hegemony. In the 2013 election, the opposition Cambodian National Rescue Party marshalled a serious challenge to the CPP's authority, and the election result was met with

[6] For a more detailed discussion of the political settlement in Cambodia, see Kelsall and Seiha (2015).

significant public demonstrations and claims of electoral fraud and corruption, particularly among dissatisfied urban youth. The CPP's response has been strongly to repress oppositional activity—with the 2018 elections dismissed by opposition activists and some observers as a sham—while also seeking to boost its legitimacy through social provisioning (Kelsall and Seiha 2015). Institutions generally have a personalistic character, although there are pockets of more rule-governed functioning within the state, offering some opportunity for rule-based reform progress (Kelsall et al. 2016: 67).

Under the stability of the post-1998 dominant settlement, Cambodia has generally seen strong economic growth and poverty reduction. The government has pursued a mixed strategy, allowing some role for technocratic branches of the state in supporting selected industries, but also often indulging rent-seekers with controversial sweetheart deals allowing them to generate profits, some of which are distributed to the mass of the population through ruling party patronage projects (Kelsall and Seiha 2015). In terms of development interventions, rapid progress tends to be found where the interests of development partners and domestic political leaders combine. For instance, expansion in education infrastructure and access satisfied both politicians' and donors' desires for easily demonstrable achievements, whether to please voters or Millennium Development Goals (MDG) assessments respectively (Kelsall et al. 2016: 10–11).

Ethiopia

Up until 2018, and for the period covered by our research, Ethiopia's dominant party settlement was led by the Ethiopian People's Democratic Revolutionary Front (EPDRF), a multi-ethnic coalition founded by the Tigrayan People's Liberation Front (TPLF) in 1989, and in power since 1991.[7] This coalition included parties in Amhara, Oromiya, and Southern Nations, Nationalities and Peoples' Region (SNNPR), but was dominated by the TPLF, despite the people of Tigray comprising only 6 per cent of the total population. Through the EPDRF's history, the coalition maintained its support through a commitment to development, economic growth, and the institutionalization of ethnic federalism. In certain respects, the EPDRF's stability enabled longer-term developmental planning, seen, for instance, in the 'Agricultural Development-Led Industrialization' (ADLI) strategy, and in the ability to implement reforms in the health sector.

While the EPRDF significantly consolidated power from rivals from the early 2000s onwards, the coalition has also fragmented, and by the early 2010s was showing increasing signs of vulnerability. In the 2005 election, the party faced a surprisingly well-organized opposition, and subsequently suffered a reduction in its parliamentary majority. During this period, opposition leaders were arrested and over 200 protestors killed, and opposition forces have since been systematically undermined. The death of TPLF chairman and long-standing prime minister Meles Zenawi in 2012 led to factionalism and a realignment within the ruling coalition away from the TPLF. This instability has weakened the coalition's ability to respond coherently to national challenges. Unemployment, food crises, and increased ethnic nationalism have all motivated serious anti-government protests, increasing the pressure on the ruling coalition to deliver public goods effectively and equitably across the ethnically federated country. Following the unexpected resignation of Zenawi's successor, the reform-minded Abiy Ahmed became prime minister in April 2018, ending the TPFL's reign and further reducing the power of centrifugal dynamics in Ethiopia's political settlement.

[7] For a more detailed discussion of the political settlement in Ethiopia, see Lavers (2019a).

Rwanda

Contemporary Rwanda presents a clear example of a dominant-party political settlement.[8] The Rwandan Patriotic Front (RPF) emerged as the country's dominant political force following the 1994 genocide, and, since then, under the leadership of Paul Kagame, has consolidated control over both government and society. The RPF and the president receive widespread support from the military, and retain a highly militarized character in terms of mindset and operating principles, while facing no significant competition from either elite or lower-level factions. In developmental terms, Rwanda can boast significant achievements, with transparent public-sector investment and relatively efficient government performance, evidenced by, for example, the highest enrolment in health insurance in sub-Saharan Africa. Such achievements are all the more striking when compared to the condition of some of Rwanda's neighbours, such as Uganda and Burundi (Chemouni 2017).

Rwanda's ability to deliver such development outcomes relates to the nature of its political settlement (Booth and Golooba-Mutebi 2012; Goodfellow 2014). Beneath the surface there is more complexity here. Despite the organizational strength of the RPF, and the apparent lack of any political challenge on the horizon, the party retains in some sense a latent vulnerability in that it constitutes a predominantly ethnically Tutsi organization ruling a country whose population is ethnically Hutu in the large majority (around 85 per cent). Wary of the hostilities that its own existence grew out of, the RPF has been careful to cultivate a sense that the social base of the settlement is broad, by including (albeit arguably in less pivotal positions) some Hutu figures in a regime that might otherwise face charges of Tutsi domination from a still sometimes suspicious public (Chemouni 2017: 21–2). More generally, the RPF sees this structural backdrop as necessitating a legitimation strategy to maintain political stability; specifically, an inclusive political vision, underpinned by high modernist ideals and prizing competence and anti-corruption, has emerged as essential. Being seen to deliver both impartial governance and even developmental progress across ethnic divides, in order to avoid the return of grievances that could decimate the ruling coalition and destabilize the settlement, is a crucial aspect of this strategy. Transparency and a concerted assault on corruption have been overarching features of this project. This legitimation strategy also helps to facilitate an implicit trade-off with regards to severe restrictions on political space and contestation, which the RPF approach conceptualizes as an emphasis on consensus-building and the avoidance of factionalism and conflict.

Policy formulation is centralized and influenced by political elites under the close control of Kagame himself, who has significant influence over all areas of government—influence he wields on the basis of consolidated control and support within the military and RPF (Golooba-Mutebi 2013). This strength has enabled a high degree of ownership and control over reforms and policy, such as social protection strategy (Lavers 2019b). It has also enabled a clear top-down monitoring and accountability system in the public sector, which, although clearly effective in some sectors (e.g. health) also raises questions where gains are longer term (e.g. education), and may incentivize misreporting to avoid sanctions. As a case of a dominant-party political settlement, these developmental outcomes sit alongside the perception that the government has a heavy-handed approach to civil society, the media, and political opposition, with restrictions on freedom of association and reports of unexplained deaths and disappearances of oppositional journalists or politicians (Human Rights Watch 2020).

[8] For a more detailed discussion of the political settlement in Rwanda, see Golooba-Mutebi (2013).

South Africa

Since 1994, post-apartheid South Africa has been dominated electorally by the African National Congress (ANC).[9] For this reason, it can be categorized as a dominant-type settlement. However, the picture is a little more complex, since, as Levy et al. (2015: 3–5) note, South Africa has a widely hailed democratic constitution, whose rules governing electoral competition are scrupulously followed, and elections are both hotly contested and subject to wide public interest and engagement. This suggests that the ANC's dominance is more contingent, rather than institutionalized in non-competitive structures, as in cases like the RPF's classic dominance in Rwanda or the NRM in Uganda during the era of 'no-party' politics.

Nevertheless, the de facto situation is that of a single party that continues to enjoy long-term political dominance, albeit with growing signs of competitiveness. Given that the status quo ante was a dominant white minority elite presiding over an oppressed black majority, in the post-apartheid era the ANC has a large and broad social base, taking in the black professional class, urban workers, migrant workers, rural peasants, and landless people, and many people living in poverty in the urban periphery. Today the ANC is something of a 'big tent', and its support is very diverse both geographically and ethnically. Thus, while the constitution in many ways safeguarded the economic and other privileges of the pre-existing elite, majority rule strongly disposes the ANC towards electoral success. It also means that, with many disparate groupings and interests in play, there are tendencies for policy to be pulled in multiple directions, some of them in tension with one another.

Compared to many other countries in our study, South Africa is close to being, in Levy's terms (2014), a 'sustainable democracy'—that is, crossing over from a political settlement where impersonal Weberian state functioning has largely been achieved and the rule of law is well established, to a situation where, not only are these features retained, but democracy can be said to have become truly sustainable thanks to economic changes that see greater economic inclusion and the growth of a substantial middle class. For Levy et al. (2015), it is currently an open question whether South Africa is on the cusp of this transition, and the country's stark economic inequalities present a substantial obstacle and a factor that is beginning to put well-ordered formal political institutions under strain.

A further complexity concerns subnational variation, meaning that, in particular policy domains, the national-level political settlement is often only part of the story. The 1994 constitution established a subnational level of governance with nine provinces, each with formally identical institutional arrangements. However, in reality, the legacy of the widely disparate institutional arrangements present under the apartheid regime is an important factor leading to wide variation, such that most of our South Africa research talks in terms of 'provincial political settlements'. For instance, Levy et al. (2016) compare the differing outcomes in the governance of basic education in the Western Cape and Eastern Cape provinces, finding that variations in the political make-up of the provinces affect implementation in major and differential ways.

Uganda

Uganda's political settlement rests on the power of the National Resistance Movement (NRM) and President Yoweri Museveni, who from the late 1980s and through the 1990s brought together a wide range of factions from across the country (with the exception of the north),

[9] For a more detailed discussion of the political settlement in South Africa, see Levy et al. (2015).

orientated towards a pro-growth and later pro-poor development vision.[10] After a period of civil conflict and economic collapse, this achieved political and macroeconomic stability, wide-ranging public-sector reform, and improved access to social services for most citizens. Thus, with more than three decades under Museveni and the NRM, Ugandan politics might appear to present a clear case of a dominant-type political settlement. However, the coalition began to be eroded in the early 2000s (Golooba-Mutebi and Hickey 2013), with prominent NRM factions forming an opposition group, the 'Forum for Democratic Change'. Although this opposition has been unable to overturn a ruling coalition skilled at winning elections through various means, it has changed the political calculations of the NRM, and, with it, public policy. This transition represents a shift, in political settlements terms, from a 'developmental coalition' to a 'weak dominant party' (Khan 2010). The NRM also acceded to multi-partyism from 2005 onwards, having overseen a 'no-party' system under the auspices of an all-encompassing movement politics prior to that. Since the 2006 election in particular, it has become increasingly important (in terms of regime survival) to gain the support of lower-level factions, in order to cut off potential supporters from the opposition. This has magnified the perceived importance of populist policymaking, with the president increasingly taking control of public-sector functions and distributing government largesse on a personalized basis. Appealing directly to the masses has also served as a means for Museveni to disempower regional powerbrokers and signified a shift in power away from the NRM to the personality of Museveni himself. Such competition has increased the costs of patronage in Uganda, as support and loyalty become more needed and hence valuable.

Uganda's recent development experience, then, reflects the declining capacity of a strong developmental coalition, with an increasingly personalized approach to policymaking and governance. High levels of public-sector performance have long been circumscribed, restricted to certain bureaucratic enclaves rather than part of a wider process of state-building, in part because the configuration of social power in Uganda incentivizes provisioning rather than protection pacts (unlike in Rwanda). However, even these 'pockets of effectiveness' have become subject to increased political pressure (Golooba-Mutebi and Hickey 2016). The way Uganda's political settlement translates into development outcomes is therefore complex, in line with the complexity of how that settlement is changing. The need to accommodate lower-level and excluded factions has decreased the government's ability to implement a longer-term vision for development, and has orientated policy more towards short-term goals, as well as accentuating patronage dynamics and widespread corruption.

[10] For a more detailed discussion of the political settlement in Uganda, see Golooba-Mutebi and Hickey (2013), Hickey and Izama (2016: 5–7), and Bukenya and Gøolooba-Mutebi (2019: 4–6).

APPENDIX II

Pockets of Effectiveness

Methodological Approach

This appendix briefly sets out the basis on which we measured and tracked the performance of the three types of 'pockets of effectiveness' (PoEs) discussed in Chapter 6—namely, finance ministries (particularly budget departments), central banks, and revenue authorities. Given the current absence of databases or indexes that capture relative levels of organizational performance within the state, we were forced to innovate here.

For *finance ministries*, the department most frequently identified as high performing within our expert survey was the budget department, enabling us to echo Merilee Grindle's study (1997). According to Simson and Welham (2014), the best-known international measures of budget credibility are contained within the Public Expenditure and Financial Accountability (assessment). Within this, key indicators include those on 'Aggregate expenditure outturn compared to original approved budget' and the 'Composition of expenditure outturn compared to original approved budget with two sub-indicators'. However, PEFA only runs from 2005, whereas we were interested in a longer time period, and it also tends to focus more on processes than actual outcomes, whereas we were keen to look less at how budgets were constructed and more at how they were actually delivered. To achieve this, we used the budget performance reports produced by national ministries of finance to track performance over a longer period of time. This involved looking at patterns of actual expenditure over time, including through a focus on potential periods or moments of fiscal ill-discipline, as indicated (for example) by the number, size, and timing of supplementary budgets and examples of significant divergence between predicted and actual expenditures that lacked clear explanations.

Central banks in developing countries have been charged with two major mandates in the past few decades: securing price stability through controlling inflation and securing financial stability, largely through banking supervision. While we examined both in our wider study, here we report only on price stability. Price stability over time can be tracked via IMF data, although further analysis is required to identify the extent to which changes in inflation rates are due to exogenous factors (e.g. oil price rises, droughts) rather than the failure of central banks to set and implement effective monetary policy. What is more controversial is drawing out a normative judgement that being 'effective' in maintaining inflation at a particular level, usually a low one, is necessarily the 'right' thing from a developmental perspective. Most observers agree that both significant instability and very high rates of inflation are objectively 'bad' in that they damage the prospects for economic growth and undermine the confidence of investors. However, there are major disagreements with regards to what the ideal level of inflation should be, with those in favour of a more productivist approach to development policy advocating a more expansive strategy as compared to the more hawkish position of neoliberal policy advocates. Viewed from the narrower perspective of organizational performance, our immediate job here was to identify whether a given central bank was delivering on the mandate that it had been tasked with by the government of the day, in this case with reference to the target rate of inflation. The fact that this varied across our countries (e.g. with the East African countries largely bound to single-digit targets as opposed to the often looser approach adopted in Ghana and, in particular, Zambia) meant that we could not apply a universal standard here but rather tracked performance against national policy targets over time.

The central mandate of *revenue authorities* is clear enough; however, measuring how successful a given revenue authority is at generating tax revenues is far from straightforward, in at least two important respects. First, the most frequently used indicator of performance, namely the ratio of tax-to-GDP, is limited by the fact that this is strongly shaped by the structure of the economy, with the size and nature of the informal economy a critical determinant of a country's capacity to generate domestic revenue. We instead used the 'tax-effort' metric, which accounts for the structure of the economy and offers a ratio of the actual tax collection to the predicted tax revenue. However, the second challenge here is that this metric captures the effect of tax policy as well as tax administration, whereas revenue authorities are only directly responsible for administration—that is, collecting the revenue that has been mandated for collection by tax policy as usually set by the parent ministry of finance. This meant that we also needed to track the nature of the tax regime over time, in an effort to identify whether shifts in revenue generation performance could be most plausibly linked more to either the policy or the administrative function respectively (Figure AII.1).

Our research also involved gathering data on other aspects of PoE performance, including on key indicators that could alert us as to whether or not our organizations were receiving capacity-strengthening support. The more qualitative aspects of our work, pursued via key informant interviews, involved conducting in-depth organizational biographies with a particular focus on exploring the levels of de facto as well as de jure autonomy granted to organizations over time; the nature and quality of organizational leadership; key turning points, or critical junctures in an organization's trajectory; and how organizations responded to crisis points, particularly where these seemed to be of a political nature (e.g. fiscal indiscipline resulting from electoral pressures), in order to assess organizational resilience.

Organizational type	**Indicators**	**Data sources**	**Critical episodes**
Finance ministries (particularly budget departments)	Public expenditure patterns over time (e.g. supplementary budgets)	Annual budget reports Also PEFA, Country Policy and Institutional Assessment (CPIA)	Spikes in public expenditure reforms (e.g. Public Financial Management (PFM))
Central banks: price stability	Inflation rates over time	IMF	Spikes in inflation
Revenue authorities	Tax effort	Youhou and Goujon (2017)	Trends in data

Figure AII.1 Performance indicators for case-study PoEs
Source: authors.

References

Abdulai, A.-G. (2017). 'Competitive Cientelism and the Political Economy of Mining in Ghana', ESID Working Paper No. 78. Manchester: Effective States and Inclusive Development Research Centre, University of Manchester.

Abdulai, A.-G. (2018). 'The Political Economy of Maternal Healthcare in Ghana', ESID Working Paper No. 107. Manchester: Effective States and Inclusive Development Research Centre, University of Manchester.

Abdulai, A.-G., and Mohan, G. (2019). 'The Politics of Bureaucratic 'Pockets of Effectiveness': Insights from Ghana's Ministry of Finance', ESID Working Paper No. 119. Manchester: Effective States and Inclusive Development Research Centre, University of Manchester.

Acemoglu, D., and Robinson, J. A. (2012). *Why Nations Fail: The Origins of Power, Prosperity and Poverty*. New York: Crown Business.

Acemoglu, D., and Robinson, J. A. (2019). *The Narrow Corridor: States, Societies, and the Fate of Liberty*. New York: Penguin.

Acemoglu, D., Johnson, S., and Robinson, J. A. (2001). 'The Colonial Origins of Comparative Development', *American Economic Review*, 91: 1369–1401.

Ahikire, J., and Mwiine, A. M. (2019). 'Contesting Ideas, Aligning Incentives: The Politics of Uganda's Domestic Violence Act (2010)', in S. Nazneen, S. Hickey, and E. Sifaki (eds), *Negotiating Gender Equality in the Global South: The Politics of Domestic Violence Legislation*. London: Routledge, 67–87.

Ahmed, S., Evans, T., Standing, H., and Mahmud, S. (2013). 'Bangladesh: Innovation for Universal Health Coverage 2: Harnessing Pluralism for Better Health In Bangladesh', *Lancet*, (382/9906): 1746–55.

Aiginger, K., and Rodrik, D. (2020). 'Rebirth of Industrial Policy and an Agenda for the Twenty-First Century', *Journal of Industry, Competition and Trade*, 20: 1–19.

Allah-Mensah, B., and Osei-Afful, R. (2019). 'Between Democratisation and Patronage: The Politics of Ghana's Domestic Violence Act (2007)', in S. Nazneen, S. Hickey, and E. Sifaki (eds), *Negotiating Gender Equity in the Global South: The Politics of Domestic Violence Legislation*. London: Routledge, 152–70.

Amoako-Tuffour, J., and Owusu-Ayim, J. (2010). 'An Evaluation of Ghana's Petroleum Fiscal Regime', *Ghana Policy Journal*, 4: 7–34.

Andrews, M. (2013). *The Limits of Institutional Reform in Development: Changing Rules for Realistic Solutions*. Cambridge: Cambridge University Press

Andrews, M., and Bategeka, L. (2013). 'Overcoming the Limits of Institutional Reform in Uganda', ESID Working Paper No. 27. Manchester: Effective States and Inclusive Development Research Centre, University of Manchester.

Andrews, M., Pritchett, L., and Woolcock, M. (2012). 'Escaping Capability Traps through Problem-Driven Iterative Adaptation (PDIA)', Faculty Research Working Paper Series, RWP12-036. Harvard Kennedy School, University of Harvard.

Andrews, M., Pritchett, L., and Woolcock, M. (2017). *Building State Capability*. Oxford: Oxford University Press.

Appiah, D., and Abdulai, A.-G. (2017). 'Competitive Clientelism and the Politics of Core Public Sector Reform in Ghana', ESID Working Paper No. 82. Manchester: Effective States and Inclusive Development Research Centre, University of Manchester.

Asante, K., Abdulai, A., and Mohan, G. (2021). 'The "New" Institutional Politics of Ghana's Hydrocarbon Governance', ESID Working Paper No. 169. Manchester: Effective States and Inclusive Development Research Centre, University of Manchester.

Bardhan, P. (1989). 'The New Institutional Economics and Development Theory: A Brief Critical Assessment', *World Development*, 17/9: 1389–95.

Basheka, B. C., and Sabiiti, C. K. (2011). 'Compliance to Public Procurement Reforms in Developing Countries: The Contextual Perspective from Uganda', *International Journal of Procurement Management*, 4/5: 535–48.

Basu, A. (2010). 'Introduction', in A. Basu (ed.), *Women's Movement in a Global Era*. Boulder, CO: Westview Press, 1–371.

Basu, A. (2019). 'Building Strong Alliances: The Politics of the Protection of Domestic Violence Act in India (2006)', in S. Nazneen, S. Hickey, and E. Sifaki (eds), *Negotiating Gender Equality in the Global South: The Politics of Domestic Violence Legislation*. London: Routledge, 171–90.

Bates, R. (1981). *Markets and States in Tropical Africa: The Political Basis of Agricultural Policies: With a New Preface*. Berkeley and Los Angeles: University of California Press.

Bebbington, A. (2013). 'Natural Resource Extraction and the Possibilities of Inclusive Development: Politics across Space and Time', ESID Working Paper No. 21. Manchester: Effective States and Inclusive Development Research Centre, University of Manchester.

Bebbington, A., Abdulai, A.-G., Humphreys Bebbington, D., Hinfelaar, M., and Sandborn, C. (2018). *Natural Resource Extraction and National Politics: The Challenge of Inclusive Development*. Oxford: Oxford University Press.

Béland, D. (2005). 'Ideas and Social Policy: An Institutionalist Perspective', *Social Policy & Administration*, 39/1: 1–18.

Blyth, M. (2010). 'Ideas, Uncertainty and Evolution', in D. Béland, and R. Cox (eds), *Ideas and Politics in Social Science Research*. Oxford: Oxford University Press, 1–403.

Booth, D. (2011). 'Aid Effectiveness: Bringing Country Ownership (and Politics) back in', ODI Working Paper 336. London: Overseas Development Institute.

Booth, D. (2015). 'Thinking and Working Politically', *Professional Development Reading Pack*, No.13: 1–3.

Booth, D., and Cammack, D. (2013). *Governance for Development in Africa: Solving Collective Action Problems*. London: Zed Books.

Booth, D., and Golooba-Mutebi, F. (2012). 'Developmental Patrimonialism? The Case of Rwanda', *African Affairs*, 111/444: 379–403.

Booth, D., and Unsworth, S. (2014). 'Politically Smart, Locally Led Development', ODI Discussion Paper. London: Overseas Development Institute.

Bozzini, A. (2013). *Fighting Corruption while Undermining Accountability: The Case of Rwanda*. Hamburg: German Institute of Global and Area Studies.

Brautigam, D., Fjeldstad, O. H., and Moore, M. (2008) (eds). *Taxation and State-Building in Developing Countries: Capacity and Consent*. Cambridge: Cambridge University Press.

Brooks, S. M. (2015). 'Social Protection for the Poorest: The Adoption of Antipoverty Cash Transfer Programs in the Global South', *Politics & Society*, 43/4: 551–82.

Bukenya, B., and Golooba-Mutebi, F. (2019). 'Political Settlements and the Delivery of Maternal Health Services in Rural Uganda', ESID Working Paper No. 113. Manchester: Effective States and Inclusive Development Research Centre, University of Manchester.

Bukenya, B., and Hickey, S. (2019). 'The Shifting Fortunes of the Economic Technocracy in Uganda: Caught between State-Building and Regime Survival?', ESID Working Paper No. 121. Manchester: Effective States and Inclusive Development Research Centre, University of Manchester.

Bukenya, B., and Muhumuza, W. (2017). 'The Politics of Core Sector Public Reform in Uganda: Behind the Facade', ESID Working Paper No. 85. Manchester: Effective States and Inclusive Development Research Centre, University of Manchester.

Burnet, J., and d'Arc Kanakuze, J. (2018). 'Political Settlements, Women's Representation and Gender Equality: The 2008 Gender-Based Violence Law and Gender Parity in Primary and Secondary Education in Rwanda', ESID Working Paper No. 94. Manchester: Effective States and Inclusive Development Research Centre, University of Manchester.

Burra, S., Mitlin, D., and Menon, G., with Agarwal, I., Banarse, P., Gimonkar, S., Lobo, M., Patel, S., Rao, V., and Waghmare, M. (2016). 'Understanding the Contribution of the BSUP (JNNURM) to Inclusive Cities in India', ESID Working Paper No. 97. Manchester: Effective States and Inclusive Development Research Centre, University of Manchester.

Callaghy, T. M, and Ravenhill, J. (1993) (eds). *Hemmed in: Responses to Africa's Economic Decline*. New York: Columbia University Press.

Cammett, M. C. and MacLean, L. M. (2011). 'Introduction: The Political Consequences of Non-State Social Welfare in the Global South', *Studies in Comparative International Development*, 46/1: 1–21.

Campioni, M., and Noack, P. (2012). *Rwanda Fast Forward: Social, Economic, Military and Reconciliation Prospects*. London: Palgrave Macmillan.

Caney, S. (2006). 'Global Justice: From Theory to Practice', *Globalizations*, 3/2: 121–37.

Carbone, G. (2009). 'The Consequences of Democratization', *Journal of Democracy*, 20/2: 123–37.

Carothers, T. D., and de Gramont, D. (2013). *Development Aid Confronts Politics: The Almost Revolution*. New York: Carnegie Endowment for International Peace.

Centeno, M. A., Kohli, A., and Yashar, D. J. (2017). *States in the Developing World*. Cambridge: Cambridge University Press.

Chemouni, B. (2017). 'The Politics of Core Public Sector Reform in Rwanda', ESID Working Paper No. 88. Manchester: Effective States and Inclusive Development Research Centre, University of Manchester.

Chemouni, B. (2019). 'The Rise of the Economic Technocracy in Rwanda: A Case of a Bureaucratic Pocket of Effectiveness or State-Building Prioritisation?', ESID Working Paper No. 120. Manchester: Effective States and Inclusive Development Research Centre, University of Manchester.

Chemouni, B., and Hossain, N. (2016). 'The Origins and Implications of Elite Commitment for Inclusive Development', ESID Evidence to Theory Paper. Manchester: Effective States and Inclusive Development Research Centre, University of Manchester.

Craig, D., and Porter, D. (2006). *Development beyond Neoliberalism: Governance, Poverty Reduction and Political Economy*. London: Routledge.

Dafe, F. (2019). 'Ambiguity in International Finance and the Spread of Financial Norms: The Localization of Financial Inclusion in Kenya and Nigeria', *Review of International Political Economy*, 27/3: 500–24.

Deacon, B. (2003). 'Global Social Governance Reform', GASPP Policy Brief, No. 1 (January), http://www.gaspp.org/publications/brief1_summary.htm (accessed on 1.10. 2022).

Deaton, A., and Cartwright, N. (2018). 'Understanding and Misunderstanding Randomised Control Trials', *Social Science and Medicine*, 210: 2–21.

Debrah, E. (2009). 'The Economy and Regime Change in Ghana, 1992–2004', *Ghana Social Science Journal*, (5–6/1–2): 84–113.

Dépelteau, F. (2013). 'What Is the Direction of the "Relational Turn"?', in C. Powell and F. Dépelteau (eds), *Conceptualizing Relational Sociology*. Basingstoke: Palgrave Macmillan.

Devereux, S., and Ulrichs, M. (2015). 'Stakeholder Perceptions on Graduation in Ethiopia and Rwanda', *IDS Bulletin*, 46/2: 145–54.

DFID (Department for International Development) (2003). *Promoting Institutional and Organizational Development.* London: DFID.

DFID (Department for International Development) (2011). *Governance Portfolio Review Summary: Summary Review of DFID's Governance Portfolio 2004–2009.* London: DFID.

DFID (Department for International Development) (2017). *Economic Development Strategy: Prosperity, Poverty and Meeting Global Challenges.* London: DFID.

di John, J., and Putzel, J. (2009). 'Political Settlements: Issues Paper', Discussion Paper. Birmingham: University of Birmingham.

DLP (Development Leadership Programme) (2012). *Coalitions in the Politics of Development: A Research and Policy Workshop Report.* Birmingham: Development Leadership Programme, University of Birmingham.

Doner, R. F., and Ross Schneider, B. (2016). 'The Middle-Income Trap: More Politics than Economics', *World Politics*, 68/4: 608–44.

Doner, R. F., Ritchie, B., and Slater, D. (2005). Systemic Vulnerability and the Origins of Developmental States: Northeast and Southeast Asia in Comparative Perspective. *International Organization*, 59/2: 327–61.

Druckman, J. N., Greene, D. P., Kuklinski, J. H., and Lupia, A. (2011). 'Experimentation in Political Science', in J. N. Druckman, D. P. Green, J. H. Kuklinski, and A. Lupia (eds), *Cambridge Handbook of Experimental Political Science.* Cambridge: Cambridge University Press, 3–12.

Escobar-Lemmon, M. C., and Taylor-Robinson, M. M. (2014) (eds). *Representation: The Case of Women.* New York: Oxford University Press.

Evans, P. (1995). *Embedded Autonomy: States and Industrial Transformation.* Princeton: Princeton University Press.

Evans, P., and Heller, P. (2015). 'Human Development, State Transformation and the Politics of the Developmental State', in S. Leibfried et al. (eds), *The Oxford Handbook of Transformations of the State.* Oxford: Oxford University Press, 691–713.

Fjeldstad, O. H., and Moore, M. (2009). 'Revenue Authorities and Public Authority in Sub-Saharan Africa', *Journal of Modern African Studies*, 47/1: 1–18.

Fligstein, N., and McAdam, D. (2015). *A Theory of Fields.* Oxford: Oxford University Press.

Fosu, A. (2017). 'Oil and Ghana's Economy', in E. Aryeetey and R. Kanbur (eds), *The Economy of Ghana Sixty Years after Independence.* Oxford: Oxford University Press, 137–56.

Fraser, N. (2008). *Scales of Justice: Reimagining Political Space in a Globalizing World.* Cambridge: Polity Press.

Frederiksen, T. (2017). 'Corporate Social Responsibility and Political Settlements in the Mining Sector in Ghana, Zambia and Peru', ESID Working Paper No. 74. Manchester: Effective States and Inclusive Development Research Centre, University of Manchester.

Fritz, V., Levy, B., and Ort, R. (2014). *Problem-Driven Political Economy Analysis: The World Bank's Experience. Directions in Development—Public Sector Governance.* Washington: World Bank.

Fukuyama, F. (2013). 'What Is Governance?', *Governance*, 26/3: 347–68.

Fukuyama, F. (2016). *The Origins of Political Order.* New York: Profile Books.

Gary, I. (2009). *Ghana's Big Test: Oil's Challenge to Democratic Development.* London: Oxfam America & Integrated Social Development Centre.

George, A. L., and Bennett, A. (2005). *Case Studies and Theory Development in the Social Sciences.* Cambridge, MA: MIT Press.

Ghana MoH (Ministry of Health) (2015). *The Health Sector Medium-Term Development Plan, 2014–2017.* Accra: Ministry of Health.

Global Integrity (2011). 'Uganda 2011'. Washington, https://www.globalintegrity.org/resource/gir2011-report-uganda/ (accessed on 1.10.2022).

Global Witness (2014). 'A Good Deal Better? Uganda's Secret Oil Contracts Explained', Report, https://www.globalwitness.org/en/reports/good-deal-better/ (accessed on 1.10.2022).

Goetz, A. M. (2019). 'From Transformative Policy to Transforming Political Settlements', in S. Nazneen, S. Hickey, and E. Sifaki (eds), *Negotiating Gender Equity in the Global South: The Politics of Domestic Violence Legislation*. London: Routledge, 221–30.

Goetz, A. M., and Hassim, S. (2003) (eds). *No Shortcuts to Power: African Women in Politics and Policy-Making*. London: Zed Books.

Goldstone, J. A. (2004). 'More Movements or Fewer? Beyond Political Opportunity Structures to Relational Fields', *Theory and Society*, 33: 333–65.

Goldsworthy, D. (1988). 'Thinking Politically about Development', *Development and Change*, 19/3: 505–30.

Golooba-Mutebi, F. (2013). 'Politics, Political Settlements and Social Change in Post-Colonial Rwanda', ESID Working Paper No. 24. Manchester: Effective States and Inclusive Development Research Centre, University of Manchester.

Golooba-Mutebi, F., with Habiyonizeye, Y. (2018). 'Delivering Maternal Health Services in Rwanda: The Role of Politics', ESID Working Paper No. 106. Manchester: University of Manchester. Available at www.effective-states.org.

Golooba-Mutebi, F., and Hickey, S. (2013). 'Investigating the Links between Political Settlements and Inclusive Development in Uganda: Towards a Research Agenda', ESID Working Paper No. 20. Manchester: Effective States and Inclusive Development Research Centre, University of Manchester.

Golooba-Mutebi, F., and Hickey, S. (2016). 'The Master of Institutional Multiplicity? The Shifting Politics of Regime Survival, State-Building and Democratisation in Museveni's Uganda', *Journal of Eastern African Studies*, 10/4: 601–18.

Goodfellow, T. (2014). 'Rwanda's Political Settlement and the Urban Transition: Expropriation, Construction and Taxation in Kigali', *Journal of Eastern African Studies*, 8/2: 311–29.

Goodfellow, T., and Jackman, D. (2023) (eds). *Controlling the Capital: Political Dominance in the Urbanizing World*. Oxford: Oxford University Press.

Government of Uganda (2013). *Mid-Term Review of the Uganda National Development Plan: Political Economy Thematic Report*. Kampala: National Planning Authority.

Gray, H. (2016). 'Access Orders and the "New" New Institutional Economic of Development', *Development and Change*, 47/1: 51–75.

Gray, H. (2018). *Turbulence and Order in Economic Development: Institutions and Economic Transformation in Tanzania and Vietnam*. Oxford: Oxford University Press.

Gray, H. (2019). 'Understanding and Deploying the Political Settlements Framework', in N. Cheeseman, E. Bertrand, and S. Husaini (eds), *A Dictionary of African Politics*. Oxford: Oxford University Press.

Grindle, M. S. (1997). 'Divergent Cultures?: When Public Organizations Perform Well in Developing Countries', *World Development*, 25/4: 481–95.

Grindle, M. S. (2002) 'Despite the Odds: The Political Economy of Social Sector Reform in Latin America', in C. Abel and C. M. Lewis (eds), *Exclusion and Engagement: Social Policy in Latin America*. London: Institute of Latin American Studies, 83–110.

Grindle, M. S. (2004). 'Good Enough Governance: Poverty Reduction and Reform in Developing Countries', *Governance: An International Journal of Policy, Administration, and Institutions*, 17/4: 525–48.

Grindle, M. S. (2012). *Jobs for the Boys: Patronage and the State in Comparative Perspective*. Cambridge, MA: Harvard University Press.

Grindle, M. S. (2017). 'Good Governance, R.I.P.: A Critique and an Alternative', *Governance*, 30/1: 17–22.

Grzymala-Busse, A. (2008). 'Beyond *Clientelism*: Incumbent State Capture and State Formation', *Comparative Political Studies*, 41/4–5: 638–73.

Haggard, S. (2018). *Developmental States*. Cambridge: Cambridge University Press.

Hall, P. A. (1993). 'Policy Paradigms, Social Learning, and the State: The Case of Economic Policymaking in Britain', *Comparative Politics*, 25: 275–96.

Hall, R., and Jones, C. (1999). 'Why do Some Countries Produce So Much More Output per Worker than Others?', *Quarterly Journal of Economics*, 114: 83–116.

Hanlon, J., Barrientos, A., and Hulme, D. (2010). *Just Give Money to the Poor: The Development Revolution from the Global South*. Sterling, VA: Kumarian.

Harrison, G. (2010). *Neoliberal Africa: The Impact of Global Social Engineering*. London: Zed Books.

Hassan, M. (2013). 'Political Settlement Dynamics in a Limited-Access Order: The Case of Bangladesh', ESID Working Paper No. 23. Manchester: Effective States and Inclusive Development Research Centre, University of Manchester.

Hassan, M., and Raihan, S. (2017). 'Navigating the Deals World: The Politics of Economic Growth in Bangladesh', in L. Pritchett, K. Sen, and E. Werker (eds), *Deals and Development: The Political Dynamics of Growth Episodes*. Oxford: Oxford University Press, 96–128.

Hay, C. (2011). 'Ideas and the Construction of Interests', in D. Béland and R. H. Cox (eds), *Ideas and Politics in Social Science Research*. Oxford: Oxford University Press, 65–82.

Heller, P. (2013). 'Challenges and Opportunities: Civil Society in a Globalizing World', UNDP–HDRO Occasional Papers No. 2013/06. United Nations Development Programme.

Heller, P., and Evans, P. (2010). 'Taking Tilly South: Durable Inequalities, Democratic Contestation, and Citizenship in the Southern Metropolis', *Theory and Society*, 39/3–4: 433–50.

Herbst, J. (2000). *States and Power in Africa: Comparative Lessons in Authority and Control*. Princeton: Princeton University Press.

Hertog, S. (2010). 'Defying the Resource Curse: Explaining Successful State-Owned Enterprises in Rentier States', *World Politics*, 62/2: 261–301.

Hickey, S. (2008). 'Conceptualising the Politics of Social Protection in Africa', in A. Barrientos and D. Hulme (eds), *Social Protection for the Poor and Poorest: Concepts, Policies and Politics*. London: Palgrave.

Hickey, S. (2013). 'Beyond the Poverty Agenda? Insights from the New Politics of Development in Uganda', *World Development*, 43: 194–206.

Hickey, S. (2014). 'Relocating Social Protection within a Radical Project of Social Justice: Towards a Relational Approach', *European Journal of Development Research*, 26/3: 322–37.

Hickey, S. (2019). 'The Politics of State Capacity and Development in Africa: Reframing and Researching "Pockets of Effectiveness"', ESID Working Paper No. 117. Manchester: Effective States and Inclusive Development Research Centre, University of Manchester.

Hickey, S. (2023a) (ed.). *Pockets of Effectiveness and the Politics of State-Building and Development in Africa*. Oxford: Oxford University Press.

Hickey, S. (2023b). 'The Politics of Taxation in Uganda: The Role of the Uganda Revenue Authority', ESID Working Paper. Manchester: Effective States and Inclusive Development Research Centre, University of Manchester.

Hickey, S., and Bukenya, B. (2019a). 'The Politics of Promoting Social Cash Transfers in Uganda', *Development Policy Review*, 39/1: 1–20.

Hickey, S., and Bukenya, B. (2019b). 'The Politics of Promoting Social Protection in Uganda: A Comparative Analysis of Social Cash Transfers and Social Health Insurance', in S. Hickey, T. Lavers, M. Niño-Zarazúa, and J. Seekings (eds), *The Politics of Social Protection in Eastern and Southern Africa*. Oxford: Oxford University Press, 202–24.

Hickey, S., and Hossain, N. (2019) (eds). *The Politics of Education in Developing Countries: From Schooling to Learning*. Oxford: Oxford University Press.

Hickey, S., and Izama, A. (2016). 'The Politics of Governing Oil in Uganda: Going against the Grain?', *African Affairs*, 116/463: 163–85.

Hickey, S., and Izama, A. (2020). 'The Politics of Governing Oil after "Best-Practice" Reforms: Can "Pockets of Effectiveness" Survive within Uganda's Political Settlement?', *Extractive Industries and Society*, 7/4: 1200–10, https://doi.org/10.1016/j.exis.2020.05.011.

Hickey, S., and Matsiko, H. (2023). 'The Politics of Central Banking in Uganda: Exploring the Rise and Fall of Uganda's Premier "Pocket of Effectiveness"', ESID Working Paper. Manchester: Effective States and Inclusive Development Research Centre, University of Manchester.

Hickey, S., and Seekings, J. (2017). *The Global Politics of Social Protection*, UNU–Wider Working Paper 2017/115. Helsinki: UNU–Wider.

Hickey, S., and Seekings, J. (2019). 'Who Should Get What, How and Why? DfID and the Transnational Politics of Social Cash Transfers', in S. Hickey, T. Lavers, M. Niño-Zarazúa, and J. Seekings (eds), *The Politics of Social Protection in Eastern and Southern Africa*. Oxford: Oxford University Press.

Hickey, S., Sen, K., and Bukenya, B. (2015) (eds). *The Politics of Inclusive Development: Interrogating the Evidence*. Oxford: Oxford University Press.

Hickey, S., Lavers, T., Niño-Zarazúa, M., and Seekings, J. (2019) (eds). *The Politics of Social Protection in Eastern and Southern Africa*. Oxford: Oxford University Press.

Hickey, S., Abdulai, A.-G., Izama, A., and Mohan, G. (2020). 'Responding to the Commodity Boom with Varieties of Resource Nationalism: Explaining the Different Routes Taken by Africa's New Oil Producers', *Extractive Industries and Society*, 7/4: 1246–56.

Hidalgo, C. A., and Hausmann, R. (2009). 'The Building Blocks of Economic Complexity', *Proceedings of the National Academy of Science*, 106/26: 10570–5.

Hinfelaar, M, and Achberger, J. (2017). 'The Politics of Natural Resource Extraction in Zambia', ESID Working Paper No. 80. Manchester: Effective States and Inclusive Development Research Centre, University of Manchester.

Hinfelaar, M., and Cheelo, C. (2021). 'The Growth of Zambia Revenue Authority amidst Changing Political Coalitions in Zambia, 1994–2019', ESID Working Paper No. 171. Manchester: Effective States and Inclusive Development Research Centre, University of Manchester.

Hinfelaar, M., and Sichone, J. (2019). 'The Challenge of Sustaining a professional Civil Service amidst Shifting Political Coalitions: The Case of the Ministry of Finance in Zambia, 1991–2018', ESID Working Paper No. 122. Manchester: Effective States and Inclusive Development Research Centre, University of Manchester.

Hossain, N. (2017). *The Aid Lab: Understanding Bangladesh's Unexpected Economic Success*. Oxford: Oxford University Press.

Hout, W. (2013). 'Neo-Patrimonialism and Development: Pockets of Effectiveness as Drivers of Change', *Revue internationale de politique comparée*, 20: 79–96.

Human Rights Watch (2020). 'Rwanda' (Country Chapter), in *HRW World Report 2020*, https://www.hrw.org/world-report/2020/country-chapters/rwanda.

Humphreys, M., Sachs, J. D., and Stiglitz, J. E. (2007) (eds). *Escaping the Resource Curse*. New York: Colombia University Press.

Hutchful, E. (1997). 'The Institutional and Political Framework of Macro-Economic Management in Ghana', UNRISD Discussion Paper 82. Geneva: UNRISD.

ILO (International Labour Organization) (2014). *World Social Protection Report 2014/15: Building Economic Recovery, Inclusive Development and Social Justice*. Geneva: ILO.

IMF (International Monetary Fund) (2005). *World Economic Outlook*. Washington: IMF.

IMF (International Monetary Fund) (2014). 'Second Review under the Policy Support Instrument and Request for Modification of Assessment Criteria—Staff Report; Press Release; and Statement by the Executive Director for Uganda', Uganda Country Report No. 14/195. Washington: IMF.

International Budget Partnership (2012). 'Open Budget Index 2012: Ghana', https://www.internationalbudget.org/wp-content/uploads/OBI2012-GhanaCS-English.pdf.

Jackson, C. (2003). 'Gender Analysis of Land: Beyond Land Rights for Women?', *Journal of Agrarian Change*, 3/4: 453–80.

Jackson, R. H. (1993). *Quasi-States: Sovereignty, International Relations, and the Third World*. Cambridge Studies in International Relations. New York: Cambridge University Press.

Jackson, R. H., and Rosberg, C. G. (1982). 'Why Africa's Weak States Persist: The Empirical and the Juridical in Statehood', *World Politics*, 35/1: 1–24.

Jepson, N. (2020). *In China's Wake: How the Commodity Boom Transformed Development Strategies in the Global South*. New York: Columbia University Press.

Jessop, B. (2007). *State Power: A Strategic–Relational Approach*. Cambridge: Polity Press.

Johnson, C. (1982). *MITI and the Japanese Miracle: The Growth of Industrial Policy, 1925–1975*. Stanford: Stanford University Press.

Jones, B. F., and Olken, B. A. (2008). 'The Anatomy of Start Stop Growth', *Review of Economics and Statistics*, 90/3: 582–7.

Kar, S., Pritchett, L., Raihan, S., and Sen, K. (2013). *The Dynamics of Economic Growth: A Visual Handbook of Growth Rates, Regimes, Transitions and Volatility*. Manchester: Effective States and Inclusive Development Research Centre, University of Manchester.

Karl, T. (2007). 'Ensuring Fairness: The Case for a Transparent Fiscal Social Contract', in M. Humphreys, J. Sachs, and J. Stiglitz (eds), *Escaping the Resource Curse*. New York: Columbia University Press.

Kashambuzi, R. J. (2010). *The Story of Petroleum Exploration in Uganda: 1984–2008: A Matter of Faith*. Kampala: IMPRO Publications Ltd.

Kelsall, T. (2014). 'Authoritarianism, Democracy, and Development: State of the Art', Paper 03. Birmingham: Developmental Leadership Programme, University of Birmingham.

Kelsall, T. (2018). 'Towards a Universal Political Settlement Concept: A Response to Mushtaq Khan', *African Affairs*, 117/469: 656–69, https://doi.org/10.1093/afraf/ady018 (accessed on 1.10.2022).

Kelsall, T. (2020). 'Political Settlements and the Implementation of Maternal Health Policy in the Developing World: A Comparative Case Study of Rwanda, Ghana, Uganda and Bangladesh', ESID Working Paper No. 137. Manchester: Effective States and Inclusive Development Research Centre, University of Manchester.

Kelsall, T., and Seiha, H. (2015). 'Inclusive Healthcare and the Political Settlement in Cambodia', *New Political Economy*, 21/2: 238–55.

Kelsall, T., Khieng, S., Chuong, C., and Tek Muy, T. (2016.) 'The Political Economy of Primary Education Reform in Cambodia', in S. Hickey and N. Hossain (eds), *The Politics of Education in Developing Countries: From Schooling to Learning*. Oxford: Oxford University Press, 132–151.

Kelsall, T., Khieng, S., Chuong, C., and Tek Muy, T. (2019). 'The political economy of primary education reform in Cambodia', in S. Hickey and N. Hossain (eds.), *The Politics of Education in Developing Countries: From Schooling to Learning*. Oxford: Oxford University Press, 132–151.

Kelsall, T., Schulz, N., Ferguson, D. W., Vom Hau, M., Hickey, S., and Levy, B. (2022). *Political Settlements and Development: Theory, Evidence, and Implications*. Oxford: Oxford University Press.

Khan, M. (1995). 'State Failure in Weak States: A Critique of New Institutionalist Explanations', in J. Harriss, J. Hunter, and C. Lewis (eds), *The New Institutional Economics and Third World Development*. London: Routledge, 71–86.

Khan, M. (2000). 'Rents, Efficiency and Growth', in M. Khan and K. S. Jomo (eds), *Rents, Rent-Seeking and Economic Development: Theory and Evidence in Asia*. Cambridge: Cambridge University Press, 21–69.

Khan, M. (2005). 'The Capitalist Transformation', in K. S. Jomo and E. S. Reinert (eds), *The Origins of Development Economics: How Schools of Economic Thought Have Addressed Development*. London: Zed Press, 69–80.

Khan, M. (2010). 'Political Settlements and the Governance of Growth-Enhancing Institutions, Draft Paper', Research Paper Series on 'Growth-Enhancing Governance', London: SOAS, University of London.

Khan, M. (2013). 'Bangladesh: Economic Growth in a Vulnerable LAO', in D. C. North, J. J. Wallis, S. B. Webb, and B. R. Weingast (eds), *In the Shadow of Violence: Politics, Economics and the Problems of Development*. Cambridge: Cambridge University Press, 24–69.

Khan, M. (2017). 'Political Settlements and the Analysis of Institutions', *African Affairs*, 117/469: 636–55.

Khemani, S., Dal, B. E., Ferraz, C., Finan, F. S., Stephenson, J., Corinne, L., Odugbemi, A. M., Thapa, D., and Abrahams, S. D. (2016). *Making Politics Work for Development: Harnessing Transparency and Citizen Engagement (English)*. Policy Research Reports. Washington: World Bank Group.

King, S., and Sifaki, E. (2019). 'Ending Domestic Violence: The Politics of Global Norm Diffusion', in S. Nazneen, S. Hickey, and E. Sifaki (eds), *Negotiating Gender Equality in the Global South: The Politics of Domestic Violence Legislation*. London: Routledge, 44–66.

Kjær, A. M. (2015). 'Political Settlements and Productive Sector Policies: Understanding Sector Differences in Uganda', *World Development*, 68: 230–41.

Kjær, A. M., and Muwanga, N. (2017). 'Inclusion as Political Mobilisation: The Political Economy of Quality Education Initiatives in Uganda', ESID Working Paper No. 65. Manchester Effective States and Inclusive Development Research Centre, University of Manchester.

Kjær, A. M., and Ulriksen, M., with Kangave, J., and Katusiimeh, M. (2017). 'A Political Economy Analysis of Domestic Resource Mobilization in Uganda', UNRISD Working Paper 2017–18. UNRISD.

Kimenyi, M., Mwega, F., and Ndung'u, N. (2016). *The African Lions: Kenya*. Washington: Brookings.

Kohli, A. (2004). *State-Directed Development: Political Power and Industrialisation in the Global Periphery*. Cambridge: Cambridge University Press.

Kosack, S. (2012). *The Education of Nations: How the Political Organization of the Poor, not Democracy, Led Governments to Invest in Mass Education*. Oxford: Oxford University Press.

Kpessa, M. W., and Béland, D. (2013). 'Mapping Social Policy Development in Sub-Saharan Africa', *Policy Studies*, 34/3: 326–41.

Kuteesa, F., Tumusiime-Mutebile, E., Whitworth, A., and Williamson, T. (2010). *Uganda's Economic Reforms: Insider Accounts*. Oxford: Oxford University Press.

Lavers, T. (2018). 'Taking Ideas Seriously within Political Settlements Analysis', ESID Working Paper No. 95. Manchester: University of Manchester, www.effective-states.org.

Lavers, T. (2019a). 'Social Protection in an Aspiring "Developmental State": The Political Drivers of Ethiopia's PSNP', *African Affairs*, 118/473: 646–71.

Lavers, T. (2019b). 'Understanding Elite Commitment to Social Protection: Rwanda's Vision 2020 Umurenge Programme', in S. Hickey, T. Lavers, M. Niño-Zarazúa, and J. Seekings (eds), *The Politics of Social Protection in Eastern and Southern Africa*. Oxford: Oxford University Press.

Lavers, T. (2022) (ed.). *The Politics of Distributing Social Transfers: State Capacity and Political Contestation in Sub-Saharan Africa and South Asia.* Oxford: Oxford University Press.

Lavers, T., and Hickey, S. (2016). 'Conceptualising the Politics of Social Protection Expansion in Low-Income Countries: The Intersection of Transnational Ideas and Domestic Politics', *International Journal of Social Welfare*, 25/4: 388–98.

Lavers, T., and Hickey, S. (2021). 'Alternative Routes to the Institutionalisation of Social Transfers in Sub-Saharan Africa: Political Survival Strategies and Transnational Policy Coalitions', World Development, 146, 105549.

Leftwich, A. (1994). 'Governance, the State, and the Politics of Development', *Development and Change*, 25/2: 363–86.

Leftwich, A. (1995). 'Bringing Politics back in: Towards a Model of the Developmental State', *Journal of Development Studies*, 31: 400–27.

Leftwich, A. (2005). 'Politics in Command: Development Studies and the Rediscovery of Social Science', *New Political Econom*, 10: 573–607.

Leftwich, A. (2007). 'The Political Approach to Institutional Formation, Maintenance and Change: A Literature Review Essay', IPPG Discussion Paper No. 14, www.ippg.org.uk.

Leftwich, A. (2010). 'Beyond Institutions: Rethinking the Role of Leaders, Elites and Coalitions in the Industrial Formation of Developmental States and Strategies', *Forum for Development Studies*, 37/1: 93–111.

Leftwich, A., and Wheeler, C. (2011). 'Politics, Leadership and Coalitions in Development: Findings, Insights and Guidance from the DLP's First Research and Policy Workshop', Frankfurt, 10–11 March. Birmingham: Developmental Leadership Programme, University of Birmingham.

Leonard, D. (1991). *African Successes: Four Public Managers of Kenyan Rural Development.* Berkeley and Los Angeles: University of California Press.

Leonard, D. (2008). 'Where Are "Pockets" of Effective Agencies Likely in Weak Governance States and Why? A Propositional Inventory', IDS Working Paper 306. Brighton: IDS (Institute of Development Studies).

Levi, M. (1988). *Of Rule and Revenue.* Berkeley and Los Angeles: University of California Press.

Levi, M., and Sacks, A. (2009). 'Legitimating Beliefs: Sources and Indicators', *Regulation and Governance*, 3/4: 311–33.

Levy, B. (2014). *Working with the Grain: Integrating Governance and Growth in Development Strategies.* New York: Oxford University Press.

Levy, B., and Walton, M. (2013). 'Institutions, Incentives and Service Provision: Bringing Politics back in', ESID Working Paper No. 18. Manchester: Effective States and Inclusive Development Research Centre, University of Manchester.

Levy, B., Hirsch, A., and Woolard, I. (2015). 'Governance and Inequality: Benchmarking and Interpreting South Africa's Evolving Political Settlement', ESID Working Paper No. 51. Manchester: Effective States and Inclusive Development Research Centre, University of Manchester.

Levy, B., Cameron, R., Hoadley, U. and Naidoo, V. (2018). *The Politics and Governance of Basic Education: A Tale of Two South African Provinces.* Oxford: Oxford University Press.

Lewis, P. M. (2007). *Growing Apart: Oil, Politics, and Economic Change in Indonesia and Nigeria.* Ann Arbor: University of Michigan Press.

Leys, C. (1975). *Underdevelopment in Kenya.* Nairobi, Kenya: East African Publishers.

Lindemann, S. (2011). 'Inclusive Elite Bargains and the Dilemma of Unproductive Peace: A Zambian Case Study', *Third World Quarterly*, 32: 1843–69.

Lyon, T. (1997). 'Ghana's encouraging elections: A major step forward'. *Journal of Democracy*, 8/2: 65–77.

McDermott, R. (2002). 'Experimental Methods in Political Science', *Annual Review of Political Science*, 5: 31–61.

McDonnell, E. M. (2020). *Patchwork Leviathan: Pockets of Bureaucratic Effectiveness in Developing States.* Princeton: Princeton University Press.

Macuane, J. J., Buur, L., and Monjane, C. M. (2018). 'Power, Conflict and Natural Resources: The Mozambican Crisis Revisited', *African Affairs*, 117/468: 415–38.

Mahmud, S., with Sharmeen, N., and Mahzab, M. (2020). 'Political Economy of Policy and Implementation in the Bangladesh Health Sector: Implications for Reducing Maternal Mortality', ESID Working Paper No. 133. Manchester: The University of Manchester. Available at www.effective-states.org.

Mason, N. M., Jayne, T. S., and Mofya-Mukuka, R. (2013). 'Zambia's Input Subsidy Programs', *Agricultural Economics*, 44/6: 613–28.

Médard, J.-F. (1982). 'The Underdeveloped State in Tropical Africa: Political Clientelism or Neo-Patrimonialism?', in C. Clapham (ed.), *Private Patronage and Public Power: Political Clientelism in the Modern State.* New York: St Martin's Press, 162–192.

Mehta, P., and Walton, M. (2014). 'Ideas, Interests and the Politics of Development Change in India: Capitalism, Inclusion and the State', ESID Working Paper No. 36. Manchester: Effective States and Inclusive Development Research Centre, University of Manchester.

Moe, T. (2005). 'Power and Political Institutions', *Perspectives on Politics*, 3/2: 215–33.

Mohan, G., Asante, K. P., and Abdulai, A.-G. (2018). 'Party Politics and the Political Economy of Ghana's Oil', *New Political Economy*, 23/3: 274–89.

Mosley, P. (2017). *Fiscal Policy and the Natural Resources Curse: How to Escape from the Poverty Trap.* London: Routledge.

Mosley, P., and Chiripanhura, B. (2016). 'The African Political Business Cycle: Varieties of Experience', *Journal of Development Studies*, 52/27: 917–32.

Muchai, D., and Muchai, J. (2016). 'Fiscal Policy and Capital Flight in Kenya', *African Development Review*, 28/1: 8–21.

Nazneen, S. (2017). 'Negotiating Gender Equity in a Clientelist State: The Role of Informal Networks in Bangladesh', in G. Waylen (ed.), *Gender and Informal Institutions.* London: Rowman and Littlefield International.

Nazneen, S. (2019.) 'Building Strategic Relationships with the Political Elites: The Politics of Bangladesh's Domestic Violence Act 2010', in S. Nazneen, S. Hickey, and E. Sifaki (eds), *Negotiating Gender Equality in the Global South: The Politics of Domestic Violence Legislation.* London: Routledge, 129–51.

Nazneen, S., and Hickey, S. (2019). 'How Does Politics Shape the Negotiation of Gender Equity in the Global South? A Comparative Analysis', in S. Nazneen, S. Hickey, and E. Sifaki (eds), *Negotiating Gender Equality in the Global South: The Politics of Domestic Violence Legislation.* London: Routledge, 191–213.

Nazneen, S., Hickey, S., and Sifaki, E. (2019) (eds). *Negotiating Gender Equity in the Global South: The Politics of Domestic Violence Policy.* London: Routledge.

Nelson, J. M. (2007). 'Elections, Democracy, and Social Services', *Studies in Comparative International Development*, 41/4: 79–97.

North, D. C. (1990). *Institutions, Institutional Change and Economic Performance.* Cambridge: Cambridge University Press.

North, D. C. (1998) 'Five Propositions about Institutional Change', in J. Knight and I. Sened (eds), *Explaining Social Institutions.* Ann Arbor: University of Michigan Press, 15–26.

North, D. C., Wallis, J. J., and Weingast, B. R. (2009). *Violence and Social Orders: A Conceptual Framework for Interpreting Recorded Human History.* New York: Cambridge University Press.

North, D. C., Wallis, J. J., Webb, S. B., and Weingast, B. R. (2013). *In the Shadow of Violence: Politics, Economics, and the Problems of Development.* New York: Cambridge University Press.

Norton, A., Conway, T., and Foster, M. (2001). 'Social Protection Concepts and Approaches: Implications for Policy and Practice in International Development', Working Paper No. 143. London: Centre for Aid and Public Expenditure, Overseas Development Institute.

NRGI (Natural Resource Governance Institute) (2014). *Natural Resource Charter.* 2nd edn. New York: NGRI.

Ntayi, J. M., Ngoboka, P., Mutebi, H., and Sitenda, G. (2012). 'Social Value Orientation and Regulatory Compliance in Ugandan Public Procurement', *International Journal of Social Economics*, 39/11: 900–20.

O'Donnell, G. A. (1993). 'On the State, Democratisation and Some Conceptual Problems: A Latin American View with Glances at Some Postcommunist Countries', *World Development*, 21: 1355–69.

ODI (Overseas Development Institute) (2016). *Cash Transfers: What Does the Evidence Say?* London: ODI.

Oduro, F., Awal, M., and Ashon, M. A. (2014). 'A Dynamic Mapping of the Political Settlement in Ghana', ESID Working Paper No. 28. Manchester: Effective States and Inclusive Development Research Centre, University of Manchester.

Olson, M. (1993). 'Dictatorship, Democracy, and Development', *American Political Science Review*, 87/3: 567–76.

Opalo, K. (2019). *Legislative Development in Africa: Politics and Postcolonial Legacies.* Cambridge: Cambridge University Press.

Osei, R., Ackah, C., Domfe, G., and Danquah, M. (2017). 'Political Settlements and Structural Change: Why Growth has not been Transformational in Ghana', in L. Pritchett, K. Sen, and E. Werker (eds), *Deals and Development: The Political Dynamics of Growth Episodes.* Oxford: Oxford University Press, 159–82.

Patey, L. (2017). 'A Belated Boom: Uganda, Kenya, South Sudan, and Prospects and Risks for Oil in East Africa', Working Paper No. 71. Oxford: Oxford Institute for Energy Studies, University of Oxford.

Peck, J., and Theodore, N. (2015). *Fast Policy: Experimental Statecraft at the Thresholds of Neoliberalism.* Minnesota: University of Minnesota Press.

PEFA (Public Expenditure and Financial Accountability) (2017). *Assessments: Zambia 2017*, https://www.pefa.org/assessments/zambia-2017 (accessed on 1.10.2022).

Portes, A. (2006). 'Institutions and Development: A Conceptual Re-Analysis', *Population and Development Review*, 32: 233–62.

Poteete, A. R. (2009). 'Is Development Path Dependent or Political? A Reinterpretation of Mineral-Dependent Development in Botswana', *Journal of Development Studies*, 45/4: 544–71.

Potter, D. (2000). 'Democratization, Good Governance and Development', in T. Allen and A. Thomas (eds), *Poverty and Development into the 21st Century.* Milton Keynes: The Open University and Oxford University Press, 365–382.

Pritchett, L. (2013). *The Rebirth of Education: Schooling Ain't Learning.* Washington: Center for Global Development.

Pritchett, L. (2019). 'Understanding the Politics of the Learning Crisis: Steps ahead on a Long Road', in S. Hickey and N. Hossain (eds), *The Politics of Education in Developing Countries: From Schooling to Learning.* Oxford: Oxford University Press, 197–209.

Pritchett, L., and Woolcock, M. (2004). 'Solutions when *the* Solution Is the Problem: Arraying the Disarray in Development', *World Development*, 32/2: 191–212.

Pritchett, L., Woolcock, M., and Andrews, M. (2013). 'Looking like a State: Techniques of Persistent Failure in State Capability for Implementation', *Journal of Development Studies*, 49/1: 1–

Pritchett, L., Sen, K., Kar, S., and Raihan, S. (2016). 'Trillions Gained and Lost: Estimating the Magnitude of Growth Episodes', *Economic Modelling*, 55: 279–91.

Pritchett, L., Sen, K., and Werker, E. (2017). *Deals and Development: The Political Dynamics of Growth Episodes*. Oxford: Oxford University Press.

Pruce, K., and Hickey, S. (2019). 'The Politics of Promoting Social Cash Transfers in Zambia', in S. Hickey, T. Lavers, M. Niño-Zarazúa, and J. Seekings (eds), *The Politics of Social Protection in Eastern and Southern Africa*. Oxford: Oxford University Press, 176–201.

Putzel, J. (2004). 'The Politics of Action on AIDS: A Case Study of Uganda', *Public Administration and Development: The International Journal of Management Research and Practice*, 24/1: 19–30.

Quarles van Ufford, P., Harland, C., Michelo, S., Tembo, G., Toole, K., and Wood, D. (2016). 'The Role of Impact Evaluation in the Evolution of Zambia's Cash Transfer Programme', in B. Davis, S. Handa, N. Hypher, N. Winder Rossi, P. Winters, and J. Yablonski (eds), *From Evidence to Action: The Story of Cash Transfers and Impact Evaluation in Sub-Saharan Africa*. Oxford: Oxford University Press, 197–225.

Reno, W. (1995). *Corruption and State Politics in Sierra Leone*. Cambridge: Cambridge University Press.

Republic of Ghana (2003). *The Budget Statement and Economic Policy of the Government of Ghana for the 2004 Financial Year*. Accra: Ministry of Finance and Economic Planning.

Rodrik, D. (2004). *Getting Institutions Right*. Cambridge, MA: Harvard University Press.

Rodrik, D., Subramanian, A., and Trebbi, F. (2004). 'Institutions Rule: The Primacy of Institutions over Geography and Integration in Economic Development', *Journal of Economic Growth*, 9: 131–65.

Roll, M. (2014) (ed.). *The Politics of Public Sector Performance: Pockets of Effectiveness in Developing Countries*. London: Routledge.

Ross, M. L. (2012). *The Oil Curse: How Petroleum Wealth Shapes the Development of Nations*. Princeton: Princeton University Press.

Rosser, A. (2006). 'Escaping the Resource Curse', *New Political Economy*, 11/4: 557–70.

Sandbrook, R., Edelman, M., Heller, P., and Teichman, J. (2007). *Social Democracy in the Global Periphery*. Cambridge: Cambridge University Press.

Scarritt, J. R. (2006.) 'The Strategic Choice of Multiethnic Parties in Zambia's Dominant and Personalist Party System', *Commonwealth and Comparative Politics*, 44: 234–56.

Schmidt, V. (2008). 'Discursive Institutionalism: The Explanatory Power of Ideas and Discourse', *Annual Review of Political Science*, 11: 303–26.

Schreiber, L. (2018). 'A Foundation for Reconstruction: Building the Rwanda Revenue Authority, 2001–2017', *Innovations for Successful Societies*. Princeton University, https://successfulsocieties.princeton.edu/sites/successfulsocieties/files/LS_Rwanda_Tax_Formatted_5, 29 (accessed on 1.10.2022).

Sen, K. (2013). 'The Political Dynamics of Economic Growth', *World Development*, 47: 71–86.

Sen, K., and Tyce, M. (2018). 'The Elusive Quest for High Income Status—Malaysia and Thailand in the Post-Crisis Years', *Structural Change and Economic Dynamics*, 48: 117–35.

Sen, K., Kar, S., and Sahu, P. (2014.) 'The Political Economy of Economic Growth in India, 1993–2013', ESID Working Paper No. 44. Manchester: Effective States and Inclusive Development Research Centre, University of Manchester.

Shiffman, J. (2007). 'Generating Political Priority for Maternal Mortality Reduction in Five Developing Countries', *American Journal of Public Health*, 97/5: 796–804.

Simpson, J. P. (2017). 'Do Donors Matter Most? An Analysis of Conditional Cash Transfer Adoption in Sub-Saharan Africa', *Global Social Policy*, 18/2: 143–68.

Simson, R., and Welham, B. (2014). 'Incredible Budgets: Budget Credibility in Theory and Practice', ODI Working Paper No. 400. London: Overseas Development Institute.

Slater, D. (2010). *Ordering Power: Contentious Politics and Authoritarian Leviathans in Southeast Asia*. New York: Cambridge University Press.

Soifer, H. D., and vom Hau, M. (2008). 'Unpacking the "Strength" of the State: The Utility of State Infrastructural Power', *Studies in Comparative International Development*, 43: 219–30.

Southall, R. (1999). 'Re-Forming the State? Kleptocracy and the Political Transition in Kenya', *Review of African Political Economy*, 26/79: 93–108.

Spence, M. (2008). *The Growth Report*. Washington: World Bank.

Stasavage, D. (2005). 'Democracy and Education Spending in Africa', *American Journal of Political Science*, 49: 344–5.

Sum, N.-L., and Jessop, B. (2013). *Towards a Cultural Political Economy: Putting Culture in its Place in Political Economy*. Cheltenham: Edward Elgar.

Tangri, R., and Mwenda, A. (2013). *The Politics of Elite Corruption in Africa: Uganda in Comparative African Perspective*. London and New York: Routledge.

Teichman, J. (2015). *The Politics of Inclusive Development*. Basingstoke: Palgrave Macmillan.

Thurber M. C., Hults, D. R., and Heller, P. R. (2011). 'Exporting the "Norwegian Model": The Effect of Administrative Design on Oil Sector Performance', *Energy Policy*, 39/9: 5366–78.

Tilly, C. (1975). 'Reflections on the History of European State-Making', in C. Tilly (ed.), *The Formation of National States in Western Europe*. Princeton: Princeton University Press, 3–83.

Tilly, C. (1978). *From Mobilization to Revolution*. New York: McGraw-Hill.

Tyce, M. (2020b.) 'Competition, Fragmentation and "Resource Factionalism": The Politics of Governing Oil and Gas in Kenya', ESID Working Paper No. 140. Manchester: Effective States and Inclusive Development Research Centre, University of Manchester.

Tyce, M. (2020c). 'KRA has the Capacity, but it is Kept on a Tight Leash: The Politics of Tax Administration and Policy in Kenya', ESID Working Paper No. 159. Manchester: Effective States and Inclusive Development Research Centre, University of Manchester.

UNESCO (2014) (ed.). *Teaching and Learning: Achieving Quality for All*. EFA Global Monitoring Report, 11. 2013/14. Paris: UNESCO.

UWEZO (2012). *Are Our Children Learning? Annual Learning Assessment Report*. Kampala: UWEZO Uganda.

van de Walle, N. (2001). *African Economies and the Politics of Permanent Crisis, 1979–1999*. Cambridge: Cambridge University Press.

van de Walle, N. (2016) 'Democracy Fatigue and the Ghost of Modernization Theory', in T. Hagmann and F. Reyntjens (eds), *Aid and Authoritarianism in Africa: Development without Democracy*. London: Zed Books, 161–178.

vom Hau, M. (2012). 'State Capacity and Inclusive Development: New Challenges and Directions', ESID Working Paper No. 2. Manchester: Effective States and Inclusive Development Research Centre, University of Manchester.

von Gliszczynski, M. (2015). *Cash Transfers and Basic Social Protection: Towards a Development Revolution?* Basingstoke: Palgrave Macmillan.

Vu, T. (2007). 'State Formation and the Origins of Developmental States in South Korea and Indonesia', *Studies in Comparative International Development*, 41: 27–56.

Wade, R. (1996). 'Japan, the World Bank, and the Art of Paradigm Maintenance: "The East Asian Miracle" in Political Perspective', *New Left Review*, 217: 3–36.

Wanyama, F., and McCord, A. (2017). 'The Politics of Scaling up Social Protection in Kenya', ESID Working Paper No. 87. Manchester: Effective States and Inclusive Development Research Centre, University of Manchester.

Watts, M. J. (2004). 'Antinomies of Community: Some Thoughts on Geography, Resources and Empire', *Transactions of the Institute of British Geographers*, 29: 195–216.

Waylen, G. (2007). 'Women's Mobilization and Gender Outcomes in South Africa', *Comparative Political Studies*, 40/5: 521–46.

Waylen, G. (2012). 'Gender Matters in Politics', *Political Quarterly*, 83/1: 24–32.

Waylen, G. (2014). 'Informal Institutions, Institutional Change and Gender Equality', *Political Research Quarterly*, 67/1: 212–23.

Whitfield, L., Therkildsen, O., Buur, L., and Kjær, A. M. (2015). *The Politics of African Industrial Policy: A Comparative Perspective.* Cambridge: Cambridge University Press.

Williams, T. (2017). 'Oriented towards Action: The Political Economy of Primary Education in Rwanda', ESID Working Paper No. 64. Manchester: Effective States and Inclusive Development Research Centre, University of Manchester.

World Bank (2002). *Building Institutions for Markets.* World Development Report 2002. New York: Oxford University Press.

World Bank (2008). *Public Sector Reform: What Works and Why? An IEG Evaluation of World Bank Support.* Washington: World Bank.

World Bank (2009). 'Economy-Wide Impact of Oil Discovery in Ghana', *World Bank Report No. 47321-GH*, 30 November. Washington: World Bank.

World Bank (2013). *Transforming Central Finance Agencies in Poor Countries: A Political Economy Approach.* Washington: World Bank.

World Bank (2014). *Program Appraisal Document on a Proposed Credit in the Amount SDR 5.9 million (US$100.00 Million Equivalent) to the Republic of Rwanda for a Public Governance Program-for-result. Report No. 91140-RW.* Washington, DC: World Bank.

World Bank (2015). *Implementation Completion and Results Report: Uganda Public Service Performance Enhancement Project.* Washington: World Bank.

World Bank (2017). *World Development Report 2017: Governance and Law.* Washington: World Bank.

Yanguas, P. (2017). 'Varieties of State-Building in Africa: Elites, Ideas and the Politics of Public Sector Reform', ESID Working Paper No. 89. Manchester: Effective States and Inclusive Development Research Centre, University of Manchester.

Yanguas, P., and Hulme, D. (2015). 'Barriers to Political Analysis in Aid Bureaucracies: From Principle to Practice in DFID and the World Bank', *World Development*, 74: 209–19.

Youhou, D., and Goujon, M. (2017). 'Reassessing Tax Effort in Developing Countries: A Proposal of a Vulnerability-Adjusted Tax Effort Index', Working Paper No. 186. Ferdi Working Paper. Clermont-Ferrand, France: FERDI.

Index